Harley-Davidson: Riding Through Time – The Untold Story of an American Icon

Etienne Psaila

Harley-Davidson: Riding Through Time – The Untold Story of an American Icon

Copyright © 2025 by Etienne Psaila. All rights reserved.

First Edition: **February 2025**

No part of this publication may be reproduced, distributed, or transmitted in any form or by any means, including photocopying, recording, or other electronic or mechanical methods, without the prior written permission of the publisher, except in the case of brief quotations embodied in critical reviews and certain other non-commercial uses permitted by copyright law.

ISBN: 978-1-923432-12-3

Table of Contents

1. Prologue: The Call of the Open Road
2. Humble Beginnings in Milwaukee
3. Visionaries and Founding Fathers
4. Engineering Ingenuity: Crafting a Legend
5. The Early Years: Growth, Grit, and Guts
6. Wartime Efforts: Harley-Davidson in World Conflicts
7. The Roaring Twenties: A Culture in Motion
8. Surviving the Storm: The Great Depression
9. Post-War Prosperity: Rebuilding an American Icon
10. The Rebel Years: Harley and the Counterculture Movement
11. The Rise of Custom Culture
12. Global Expansion: Beyond American Borders
13. The Evolution of Engine Technology
14. Design and Aesthetics: Form Meets Function
15. Harley in Popular Culture
16. Racing and Performance: The Competitive Edge
17. The Business of a Legend
18. Challenges in the Modern Era
19. Innovation and Tradition: A Balancing Act
20. The Rider's Legacy: Stories from the Road
21. Collecting and Preserving a Cultural Treasure
22. Customization and Community: The Harley Family
23. Cultural Impact: A Symbol of American Freedom
24. The Future of Harley-Davidson
25. Epilogue: Riding Into Tomorrow

Chapter 1: Prologue – The Call of the Open Road

In the quiet hours before dawn, when the world still slumbers beneath a blanket of darkness, a solitary motorcycle rumbles to life. Its engine's low, steady growl is not merely a sound—it is a summons, an invitation to leave behind the ordinary and embrace the extraordinary. This is the call of the open road, a siren song that has echoed through decades, stirring the hearts of countless adventurers, rebels, and dreamers. It is a call deeply interwoven with the very soul of Harley-Davidson.

For over a century, Harley-Davidson has embodied the spirit of freedom and the relentless pursuit of adventure. Born in a modest Milwaukee workshop at the turn of the 20th century, this iconic brand was built on a foundation of innovation, determination, and a profound love for the open highway. The story of Harley-Davidson is not just a chronicle of machines and mechanical marvels—it is the story of a way of life that celebrates the boundless potential of the human spirit.

Imagine riding along an endless stretch of ribbon-like asphalt, the wind whipping past, carrying with it the scents of distant landscapes and the whispers of untold stories. Each mile traveled is a journey into the heart of America, where every twist and turn reveals a new chapter of the nation's cultural tapestry. On a Harley, riders are not confined by the limitations of routine or the predictability of daily life; instead, they are liberated by the promise of discovery and the thrill of possibility.

The open road represents more than just a physical path—it is a metaphor for life's endless journey, filled with unexpected encounters, challenges, and triumphs. For many, a Harley is more than a motorcycle; it is an extension of their identity, a trusted companion that has witnessed both their greatest adventures and their quietest moments of introspection. The rumble of the engine speaks to the soul, resonating with a deep-seated desire to break free from the mundane and to explore the vast, uncharted territories of existence.

In the era before modern conveniences and digital distractions, the allure of the open road was even more potent. With no GPS to dictate the route and no smartphone to capture every moment, riders were forced to rely on intuition, local knowledge, and the serendipity of chance encounters. Each journey was an intimate dialogue with the world, a conversation between the rider and the landscapes that unfolded before them. It was a time when the journey itself was as important as the destination, and the spirit of exploration was nurtured by every mile traversed.

Harley-Davidson has long been synonymous with this sense of adventure. The brand's legacy is steeped in stories of daring escapades and epic journeys, of riders who defied convention to chase horizons and redefine what it means to be free. These tales have been passed down from generation to generation, each retelling infused with the magic of the open road—a magic that continues to inspire new generations of riders.

This prologue serves as an invitation: to step into a world where the hum of an engine is the heartbeat of freedom, and the open road is a canvas upon which dreams are painted. As you embark on this journey through the history of Harley-Davidson, prepare to discover not only the evolution of a legendary motorcycle but also the enduring allure of a lifestyle defined by courage, exploration, and the unyielding pursuit of liberty.

The call of the open road is eternal. It beckons with the promise of adventure and the assurance that every journey, no matter how long or winding, is a chance to rediscover oneself. In the chapters that follow, we will delve deeper into the origins, the innovations, and the indomitable spirit that has made Harley-Davidson a beacon of freedom on two wheels. Welcome to a voyage that celebrates the art of living on the edge—a journey where every mile is a testament to the human desire to roam, to discover, and to be forever free.

Chapter 2: Humble Beginnings in Milwaukee

In the heart of Milwaukee at the dawn of the 20th century, a modest workshop buzzed with the clatter of innovation and the determination of its founders. Long before Harley-Davidson became a household name, it was merely a spark of ambition kindled in a small, cluttered space filled with the tools, scrap metal, and the raw energy of a group of pioneers who dared to dream big.

The workshop was tucked away on a quiet street, its exterior unassuming—a far cry from the modern factories of today. Inside, the air was thick with the scent of oil and metal shavings, and every surface bore the marks of tireless experimentation. This was a place where every bolt, every engine part, was crafted by hand, where the line between passion and livelihood blurred into a relentless quest for mechanical perfection.

William S. Harley and Arthur Davidson, two young men with an unyielding spirit and a shared vision, stood at the helm of this humble operation. Their friendship, forged by common interests and a daring sense of adventure, was the bedrock upon which the company was built. Late into the nights, they huddled over blueprints and prototypes, often fueled by little more than strong coffee and an unshakeable belief in their dream. The challenges they faced were formidable: limited funds, scarce resources, and a market that was only beginning to grasp the potential of the motorized motorcycle.

The early days were marked by relentless trial and error. Every misfired engine and every failed design was a lesson in perseverance. The duo's willingness to confront and learn from their mistakes laid the foundation for a legacy built on resilience. In that cramped Milwaukee workshop, innovation was not just encouraged—it was a necessity. Each breakthrough, no matter how small, was a triumph over adversity, a step forward in the arduous journey toward crafting a machine that could one day captivate the hearts of riders around the world.

The modest beginnings of Harley-Davidson were defined by the confluence of technical ingenuity and raw determination. Amid the chaos of scattered tools and half-finished parts, the workshop resonated with the hum of possibility. Every stroke of the drafting pencil, every measured cut of metal, was an investment in a future where freedom would be forged on two wheels. In those formative moments, the Harley-Davidson spirit was born—not in the grandeur of corporate boardrooms, but in the sweat and grit of a small Milwaukee workshop.

The environment in Milwaukee itself played an integral role in shaping this early chapter. A city known for its industrious character and resilient community, Milwaukee was a microcosm of American ingenuity. The local culture, steeped in hard work and a pioneering mindset, infused the budding enterprise with a sense of purpose. The city's industrial pulse, coupled with its vibrant community of craftsmen and innovators, provided both the resources and the inspiration needed to transform dreams into reality.

As the founders navigated the inevitable hardships of starting a business in a competitive and rapidly evolving industry, their resolve was continually tested. Economic constraints, technical setbacks, and the ever-present uncertainty of the future loomed large. Yet, with every challenge they overcame, Harley-Davidson inched closer to becoming the beacon of freedom it is known as today. The lessons learned in those early struggles—about innovation, collaboration, and the importance of perseverance—would go on to define the ethos of the brand for generations.

This chapter of humble beginnings is not merely a story of mechanical assembly and entrepreneurial spirit. It is a testament to the power of vision in the face of adversity, a reminder that even the grandest legends start in the smallest of spaces. The Milwaukee workshop, with its creaking floors and time-worn tools, was the crucible in which the spirit of Harley-Davidson was forged—a spirit that would later roar across highways and inspire millions to embrace the call of the open road.

In recalling these early days, we pay homage to the tenacity and creative brilliance of Harley and Davidson. Their legacy, built on the foundation of humble beginnings, continues to echo in every rev of a Harley engine—a constant reminder that greatness often emerges from the most unassuming places.

Chapter 3: Visionaries and Founding Fathers

At the core of Harley-Davidson's legendary journey were the visionaries who saw beyond the limits of their time. In the early 1900s, when motorized vehicles were but a budding idea and the future was a canvas of endless possibilities, two individuals emerged whose passion and perseverance would forever alter the landscape of American transportation. William S. Harley and Arthur Davidson, along with their early collaborators, were more than mere inventors—they were dreamers, revolutionaries, and steadfast believers in the transformative power of engineering and freedom.

The Spark of Innovation

William S. Harley, with his meticulous mind and an engineer's eye, possessed an innate curiosity about mechanics. Even as a young man, Harley was fascinated by the inner workings of machines and the endless potential they held. His attention to detail and commitment to precision were qualities that would become synonymous with the Harley-Davidson brand. Harley's approach was methodical: every calculation, every design sketch, was imbued with a sense of purpose. He saw each component of a motorcycle not just as a mechanical part, but as a vital contributor to the harmony of a greater whole—a machine that could defy the ordinary and capture the spirit of adventure.

Arthur Davidson complemented Harley's technical prowess with his charismatic energy and relentless optimism. Davidson was the embodiment of the American spirit of daring. His ambition was not confined by the boundaries of conventional thought; he dared to dream of a world where motorcycles were not simply vehicles, but symbols of liberty and individuality. With a warm smile and a can-do attitude, Arthur was a natural leader who inspired confidence in his peers and helped cultivate a sense of unity among the fledgling team. His vision extended beyond the mechanics of riding—it was about creating a lifestyle, a community bound by the mutual love for the open road.

Ambition and Shared Values

What united these two men was not just a shared ambition to build motorcycles, but a deeper alignment of values. In an era marked by rapid industrialization and a growing hunger for mobility, Harley and Davidson saw the motorcycle as a means to break free from the constraints of the past. Their work was driven by a set of core principles: a commitment to quality, a belief in the transformative power of innovation, and an unwavering dedication to freedom.

Their ambition was both technical and philosophical. On the technical front, they were determined to engineer motorcycles that were reliable, efficient, and capable of enduring the rigors of long journeys. Their designs reflected a meticulous attention to detail—every bolt and every curve was a testament to their commitment to excellence. Yet, beyond the mechanical specifications, there was a profound belief that their creation could change lives. They envisioned a future where a Harley-Davidson was not just a mode of transport but an emblem of rebellion, a ticket to a lifestyle where one could leave behind the mundane and embrace the boundless potential of the open road.

The Collaborative Spirit

The founding of Harley-Davidson was a true collaboration. While Harley and Davidson were the central figures, they were supported by a small band of skilled craftsmen and engineers who shared their passion. In that early Milwaukee workshop, ideas flowed freely, often fueled by long nights of brainstorming and the sheer joy of building something remarkable. The atmosphere was one of mutual respect and creative camaraderie, where each contribution, no matter how modest, was valued and celebrated.

This collaborative spirit extended beyond the confines of their immediate team. As the motorcycle began to take shape, the founders were quick to engage with their local community, seeking advice and feedback from fellow enthusiasts and craftsmen. They believed that every ride, every tweak to the design, and every test on the open road was a step toward perfection. Their willingness to listen, learn, and iterate laid the groundwork for an enduring legacy built on continuous improvement and mutual trust.

A Legacy of Inspiration

The personal qualities of Harley and Davidson—Harley's precision and dedication, and Davidson's bold vision and infectious optimism—created a dynamic that went far beyond the sum of its parts. Together, they forged a path that combined technical mastery with an unyielding belief in the freedom that riding represented. Their work was infused with an almost poetic determination: a drive to transform the ordinary into the extraordinary, and in doing so, to provide a vehicle for the human spirit to soar.

As we reflect on their contributions, it becomes clear that the founding fathers of Harley-Davidson were not merely builders of motorcycles, but architects of a cultural movement. Their legacy is woven into the fabric of American history—a history of innovation, rebellion, and the relentless pursuit of freedom. The vision they nurtured in those formative years continues to inspire riders around the world, reminding us that great things are achieved when technical brilliance is coupled with a fearless dream of what could be.

In celebrating the lives and values of these early pioneers, we honor not only the genesis of an iconic brand but also the spirit of adventure that has carried Harley-Davidson from a humble workshop in Milwaukee to the hearts of millions. Their story is a tribute to the power of vision, the strength of collaboration, and the enduring belief that with passion and perseverance, even the most ambitious dreams can become a reality.

Chapter 4: Engineering Ingenuity – Crafting a Legend

In the early days of Harley-Davidson, ingenuity was more than a buzzword—it was the lifeblood of a brand determined to redefine transportation. The founders and their dedicated team of craftsmen embarked on a journey where every stroke of a wrench and every spark of inspiration was driven by a singular goal: to build a motorcycle that could withstand the challenges of both the road and time.

The Spark of Innovation

At the heart of Harley-Davidson's early breakthroughs was an insatiable curiosity and a willingness to experiment. In an era when the internal combustion engine was still in its infancy, the Harley team was already pushing the envelope. They meticulously studied engine mechanics, seeking ways to increase reliability and performance while keeping production costs manageable. This relentless pursuit of innovation led to the development of prototypes that were as much works of art as they were feats of engineering.

One of the earliest innovations was the refinement of the V-twin engine—a design that would eventually become synonymous with the Harley-Davidson name. By positioning two cylinders in a V-configuration, the engineers achieved a harmonious balance between power and smooth operation. This configuration not only provided the torque necessary for long, open-road journeys but also delivered a distinctive engine sound—a growl that would become the signature roar of Harley-Davidson motorcycles.

Design Breakthroughs That Set Harley Apart

In those formative years, every design decision was critical. The challenge was to create a machine that was robust enough to handle rough terrains yet refined enough for everyday use. To this end, the early Harley engineers experimented with various frame designs, suspension systems, and drive mechanisms. Each prototype was tested rigorously on the rugged streets of Milwaukee and beyond, with feedback from real-world rides informing every subsequent iteration.

A major breakthrough came in the form of the modular design philosophy. This approach allowed individual components to be developed and perfected independently before being seamlessly integrated into the final product. By standardizing parts and emphasizing interchangeability, Harley-Davidson was able to simplify repairs and maintenance—a crucial advantage in an era when roadside service was often a distant luxury. This modularity also paved the way for future customization, enabling riders to adapt and modify their motorcycles to suit their personal tastes and the demands of diverse terrains.

Precision Meets Passion

The fusion of technical precision and creative passion was perhaps best exemplified in the evolution of Harley's engine manufacturing process. Every engine that rolled off the assembly line was the product of painstaking attention to detail. Craftsmen worked side by side with engineers, combining traditional metalworking skills with innovative techniques that were ahead of their time. The use of precision tools and carefully measured tolerances ensured that each engine operated at peak performance, setting new standards for durability and efficiency.

This commitment to quality was not just a technical pursuit—it was a philosophical stance. The engineers understood that the reliability of their motorcycles was deeply intertwined with the freedom of the rider. A well-crafted engine meant fewer breakdowns, more miles on the open road, and a riding experience that was both exhilarating and dependable. It was this symbiosis between man and machine that laid the groundwork for the Harley-Davidson legend.

Embracing Challenges with Creativity

Innovation did not come without its challenges. Early on, the Harley team faced setbacks that could have easily derailed their ambitions. Engine failures, material shortages, and the limitations of early manufacturing techniques were constant obstacles. Yet, each challenge was met with a creative solution. For instance, when faced with inconsistent engine performance, the engineers delved deep into the principles of thermodynamics and combustion efficiency. Their rigorous experiments and relentless adjustments eventually resulted in an engine design that was not only powerful but also remarkably reliable—a critical turning point that helped establish Harley-Davidson as a serious contender in the automotive arena.

Moreover, the willingness to innovate extended beyond just the mechanical components. The overall aesthetics of the motorcycle—its bold lines, rugged contours, and unmistakable silhouette—were the results of a meticulous design process. Every curve and every angle was deliberated upon, ensuring that the motorcycle was not only a technical marvel but also an object of desire. This harmonious blend of form and function set Harley-Davidson apart from competitors, creating a brand identity that was as much about lifestyle and freedom as it was about engineering excellence.

Legacy of Ingenuity

The early engineering achievements of Harley-Davidson were more than just technical milestones—they were the building blocks of a cultural phenomenon. The innovations forged in that bustling Milwaukee workshop resonated far beyond the confines of a small factory. They sparked a passion for riding that transcended mere transportation, evolving into a movement where each machine carried a piece of the pioneering spirit of its creators.

In reflecting on these early days, one sees a legacy of ingenuity that is still at the core of Harley-Davidson today. The same spirit that drove the initial experiments in the humble workshop continues to inspire modern innovations and bold design decisions. As the brand evolved, it never lost sight of the principles that defined its beginnings: a relentless quest for perfection, a deep respect for the art of engineering, and an unwavering commitment to the freedom of the open road.

Thus, the engineering ingenuity of Harley-Davidson is not just a chapter in the annals of motorcycle history—it is a testament to what can be achieved when passion meets precision, and when the desire to create something extraordinary is matched by the determination to overcome every obstacle. This is the legend that was crafted with every bolt tightened, every engine refined, and every mile conquered on the open road.

Chapter 5: The Early Years – Growth, Grit, and Guts

The journey of Harley-Davidson in its early years was as much about the character of its people as it was about the machines they built. Beyond the sparks of innovation and the refined designs emerging from that humble Milwaukee workshop, there was a period of rapid growth and relentless determination—a time when the company was transformed from a small-scale venture into a burgeoning symbol of American ingenuity and perseverance.

Laying the Foundation for Expansion

In the years following its initial breakthroughs, Harley-Davidson faced the daunting task of scaling up production while staying true to the ideals that had sparked its creation. The transition from a small workshop to a more structured operation was marked by long hours, sleepless nights, and a never-ending commitment to excellence. As word spread about the reliability and performance of these early motorcycles, demand began to grow beyond the confines of local enthusiasts. Yet with opportunity came the harsh reality of limited resources.

The founders, ever resourceful, turned each obstacle into a stepping stone. They adapted their manufacturing processes to meet increasing demand, often improvising with what was available. Repurposed tools, repainted walls, and even makeshift assembly lines became common sights as the team worked tirelessly to fill orders. This period was characterized by an admirable willingness to learn on the fly, a spirit of adaptability that would later become a cornerstone of the Harley-Davidson identity.

The Challenges of a Changing Landscape

Growth was not without its challenges. The early 20th century was a time of rapid industrial change, and Harley-Davidson found itself in the midst of a competitive and evolving market. Economic fluctuations, technological uncertainties, and even occasional setbacks in production threatened to stall progress. Financial constraints were a constant companion; every new machine built demanded not only time and skill but also a careful balancing of expenses.

Yet, these trials only served to fortify the resolve of the Harley-Davidson team. Each setback was met with a mix of grit and guts—a determination to push forward regardless of the odds. Whether it was sourcing better materials, refining production techniques, or innovating new ways to manage an expanding workforce, the company's leaders refused to let adversity define their journey. Instead, they saw each challenge as an opportunity to grow, both as a business and as a community of like-minded individuals.

Embracing a Spirit of Innovation

Amidst the struggle for expansion, innovation continued to drive the company forward. The lessons learned during those early, makeshift days in Milwaukee informed every decision. With every iteration of their motorcycles, the engineers and craftsmen honed not only their technical skills but also their ability to think creatively under pressure. New manufacturing methods were introduced—methods that would later set the standard for the industry. The emphasis on quality over quantity ensured that, even as production scaled up, each Harley-Davidson motorcycle remained a symbol of superior craftsmanship and reliability.

This period of growth was also one of community-building. The early riders and local enthusiasts became part of a broader narrative—a living testament to the brand's promise of freedom and adventure. Informal gatherings, local races, and spirited discussions about mechanical improvements helped forge a strong network of support around the brand. Every ride, every test on the road, added another layer to the growing legend of Harley-

Davidson, reinforcing the bond between the company and its riders.

The Resilience of a Brand in Formation

The formative years were not just about expansion in a commercial sense; they were about establishing a legacy. Harley-Davidson was beginning to define what it meant to be a motorcycle manufacturer in America—a company built on determination, innovation, and the belief that every machine they built was a gateway to freedom. This era was a crucible, where the raw elements of ambition, skill, and perseverance were fused together. It was a time when the founders and their team demonstrated that true growth comes not from avoiding difficulties, but from facing them head-on with unyielding courage.

In retrospect, the early expansion of Harley-Davidson stands as a testament to what can be achieved with passion and persistence. The grit of those early days—marked by innovation in the face of limited resources, and a refusal to be deterred by the inevitable challenges of a growing business—laid the groundwork for a legacy that continues to inspire. The journey was never smooth, and the road was often fraught with obstacles, but every hardship overcome contributed to the strength and character of the brand.

A Legacy Cemented by Perseverance

As Harley-Davidson evolved from a small Milwaukee workshop into a recognizable name across America, the lessons of those formative years remained ever-present. The challenges encountered during the early expansion—financial constraints, technological hurdles, and fierce competition—were met with a spirit that was unbreakable. This resilience not only enabled the company to survive but also allowed it to thrive in a rapidly changing world.

The early years of growth, grit, and guts are a powerful reminder that the path to greatness is rarely smooth. They serve as an enduring testament to the idea that with determination, resourcefulness, and a fearless attitude, even the most daunting obstacles can be transformed into opportunities. This period of Harley-Davidson's history is more than just a chapter in a business saga—it is a story of human endeavor, a tribute to the spirit of adventure that has fueled the brand from its inception and continues to resonate on every open road.

Chapter 6: Wartime Efforts – Harley-Davidson in World Conflicts

When the engines of global conflict roared to life, Harley-Davidson answered the call of duty. Both World War I and World War II marked transformative periods for the company, during which military contracts not only redefined the purpose of its machines but also reshaped the very fabric of the brand. In these turbulent times, Harley-Davidson evolved from a symbol of freedom on the open road into a vital component of national defense, its rugged motorcycles proving their worth in the most demanding of conditions.

Mobilizing for World War I

As the world plunged into the chaos of World War I, Harley-Davidson quickly recognized the opportunity—and the obligation—to contribute to the war effort. The company's robust, reliable motorcycles were ideally suited to the challenges of wartime logistics. In an era when speed, versatility, and endurance were paramount, Harley-Davidson's machines were adapted to serve as crucial tools for reconnaissance, communication, and courier duties on the battlefields of Europe.

During this period, Harley-Davidson secured military contracts that required not only rapid production increases but also modifications to meet the specific needs of soldiers in combat. Engineers and mechanics worked around the clock, fine-tuning engines for enhanced performance in harsh environments and rugged terrains. The motorcycles were often fitted with special equipment, including racks for carrying ammunition and communication gear, transforming them into mobile units capable of traversing unpredictable battle lines.

The wartime experience of World War I instilled in Harley-Davidson a newfound appreciation for the resilience of their designs. The rigorous demands of the military pushed the company to innovate under pressure, laying the groundwork for a legacy of engineering excellence that would serve it well in the decades to come. Moreover, the relationship forged with the military during these early conflicts provided valuable insights into large-scale manufacturing and logistical coordination—skills that would become indispensable during later crises.

Transformation During World War II

The outbreak of World War II presented an even greater challenge, both in scale and complexity. Once again, Harley-Davidson's reputation for rugged, dependable motorcycles caught the attention of military planners. Recognizing the vital role that fast, durable transport played in modern warfare, the company was tasked with producing a fleet of machines that could navigate not only urban battlefields but also the treacherous terrains of foreign lands.

In preparation for the war, Harley-Davidson retooled its factories and reimagined its production processes. The focus shifted from civilian leisure riding to the urgent needs of military operations. This transformation was not without its hurdles. The company had to contend with material shortages, rapidly changing specifications, and the enormous logistical demands of supplying an armed force engaged on multiple fronts. Yet, driven by the same spirit of determination that had characterized its early years, Harley-Davidson met these challenges head-on.

The motorcycles manufactured during World War II were engineered for maximum durability and versatility. They were adapted to carry heavy loads, traverse rough and unpredictable terrains, and operate in a wide range of environmental conditions—from the frozen landscapes of Europe to the humid jungles of the Pacific. Each machine that rolled off the assembly line was a testament to the company's ability to innovate under extreme pressure, with every modification meticulously designed to ensure reliability and performance in combat situations.

The Impact of Military Contracts on Evolution

Military contracts during both world wars had a profound and lasting impact on Harley-Davidson's evolution. The high-pressure environment of wartime production accelerated technological advances and forced the company to adopt new manufacturing techniques that increased efficiency and consistency. These improvements were not confined to the duration of the wars; they became integral to the company's operations in peacetime as well.

The collaboration with the military introduced a level of standardization and quality control that would define the modern Harley-Davidson motorcycle. The lessons learned on the factory floor during the war—about precision engineering, modular design, and the importance of rugged reliability—helped the company refine its product line for civilian use once the conflicts had ended. The military's rigorous testing protocols also provided valuable feedback, ensuring that the motorcycles were battle-ready before being released onto the market.

Moreover, the wartime experience left an indelible mark on the culture of Harley-Davidson. The camaraderie forged during these testing and production phases, as workers and engineers rallied together in the face of adversity, translated into a deep-seated pride that continues to be a hallmark of the brand. This sense of purpose and unity under pressure not only strengthened the company internally but also resonated with the post-war public, eager to embrace symbols of resilience and innovation.

A Legacy of Service and Innovation

Harley-Davidson's involvement in World War I and World War II transformed the company in unexpected ways. The trials of war accelerated technological innovation, honed manufacturing expertise, and reinforced the core values of durability, dependability, and freedom that had always defined the brand. The motorcycles that once carried soldiers into battle later became cherished relics of a bygone era, symbols of a time when machines were not merely built for leisure but for the survival and advancement of a nation.

As the dust settled on the battlefields, Harley-Davidson emerged from the crucible of war with a renewed sense of purpose. The lessons learned in the heat of conflict continued to influence its designs, ensuring that every subsequent model carried with it the spirit of resilience and the legacy of service. The company's wartime efforts remain a powerful chapter in its history—a period when Harley-Davidson not only helped shape the outcome of global conflicts but also solidified its identity as an enduring American icon.

In recounting this pivotal era, we see that the contributions of Harley-Davidson during the world wars were far more than a footnote in military history. They were a defining moment in the evolution of a brand that, even in the face of overwhelming adversity, continued to push the boundaries of engineering and human endeavor. The legacy of these wartime efforts lives on, a constant reminder that the spirit of innovation and the call of duty can drive us to achieve greatness even in the most challenging of times.

Chapter 7: The Roaring Twenties – A Culture in Motion

As the world emerged from the shadows of war and stepped into an era of exuberance and excess, Harley-Davidson found itself riding the crest of a cultural and economic wave that would redefine its identity. The Roaring Twenties, with its jazz-infused nights, economic prosperity, and a rebellious spirit, created a perfect backdrop for Harley-Davidson to transform from a rugged workhorse into an icon of style, freedom, and modernity.

The Jazz Age and the Pulse of Change

The 1920s were marked by a seismic shift in social attitudes and cultural expressions. Jazz music, with its syncopated rhythms and improvisational brilliance, captured the essence of a generation eager to break free from convention. In smoky nightclubs and speakeasies, the vibrant sound of saxophones and trumpets echoed the restless energy of the times. It was a period when innovation wasn't confined to music alone; it permeated every aspect of life, from fashion and art to the very way people moved through the world.

For Harley-Davidson, this cultural renaissance meant more than just an increase in production—it was an opportunity to shape its image. The freedom represented by the open road resonated with the carefree, experimental spirit of the Jazz Age. Motorcycle rallies and social rides became fashionable gatherings, where the thrill of the ride mingled with the allure of modernity. The brand's distinctive growl was as much a part of the era's soundtrack as the upbeat jazz tunes filling the air.

Economic Booms and Expanding Horizons

The economic boom of the twenties provided the financial fuel needed for both consumers and manufacturers to dream bigger. As disposable incomes rose, more Americans found themselves with the means to embrace leisure activities that were once reserved for the elite. Riding a Harley-Davidson began to symbolize more than just transportation—it became an expression of newfound affluence and personal freedom.

Harley-Davidson capitalized on this momentum by expanding production and refining its models to cater to a market that was as eager for style as it was for performance. With greater resources at their disposal, the company invested in modernizing its manufacturing processes, leading to more reliable and sophisticated machines. This era saw a harmonious blend of form and function, with the design of each motorcycle reflecting both technical excellence and a distinctive aesthetic appeal that spoke directly to the era's sensibilities.

A New Image of Rebellion and Independence

In the Roaring Twenties, the concept of rebellion was redefined. It wasn't solely about defying authority—it was about celebrating individuality and challenging traditional social norms. Harley-Davidson's motorcycles emerged as symbols of this new rebellious spirit. They offered an escape from the rigidity of conventional lifestyles, inviting riders to embark on adventures where the horizon was the only limit.

Advertisements and popular media of the time began to depict Harley-Davidson riders as modern-day adventurers—free spirits who broke away from the predictable routines of everyday life. This narrative struck a chord with a society that was increasingly valuing personal expression and independence. The motorcycle was no longer a mere machine; it was a statement, a portable manifesto of freedom that resonated with the energy and optimism of the era.

The Intersection of Technology, Culture, and Commerce

The influence of the Roaring Twenties on Harley-Davidson was multifaceted. Technologically, the period was a time of rapid innovation, as advances in manufacturing and engineering were driven by the demands of an expanding market. Culturally, the brand's image was elevated by its association with the spirit of jazz and the rebellious, freewheeling ethos of the time. Commercially, the economic boom allowed Harley-Davidson to establish itself as not only a manufacturer of motorcycles but also a purveyor of a distinctive lifestyle.

This convergence of technological progress and cultural dynamism set the stage for the brand's enduring legacy. Every Harley-Davidson motorcycle built during this period carried with it the imprint of an era defined by its vibrant energy and a daring optimism for the future. The motorcycles were celebrated not only for their performance on the open road but also for their role as emblems of a society in motion—a society that was unafraid to push boundaries and redefine the rules.

A Lasting Legacy of the Roaring Twenties

The Roaring Twenties left an indelible mark on Harley-Davidson, forging a connection between the brand and the ideals of freedom, innovation, and rebellion. The cultural and economic forces of the era propelled Harley-Davidson into the national spotlight, setting it on a trajectory that would influence generations of riders. This period of history became a touchstone for the brand's identity, a reminder that true innovation is born not just in the lab or the workshop, but in the vibrant interplay between culture and commerce.

In reflecting on this transformative decade, we see that the legacy of the Jazz Age endures in every rev of a Harley engine and every mile traveled on an open road. It is a legacy defined by the joy of movement, the thrill of discovery, and the perpetual quest for a life unbound by convention. The Roaring Twenties, with all its glamour and grit, remains a testament to a time when Harley-Davidson not only rode the winds of change but helped shape them, forever imprinting its spirit on the tapestry of American culture.

Chapter 8: Surviving the Storm – The Great Depression

When the Great Depression swept across America, it brought with it a wave of uncertainty, economic hardship, and profound challenges that tested the mettle of every business. For Harley-Davidson, a brand built on the promise of freedom and adventure, these lean times demanded not only resilience but also a willingness to reinvent the very essence of its operation. The story of Harley-Davidson during this era is one of grit, adaptation, and the unyielding spirit of survival.

The Impact of Economic Hardship

The early 1930s were a time of widespread financial strain. Banks failed, jobs were lost, and disposable incomes plummeted, leaving many Americans unable to afford luxuries, let alone a motorcycle. For a company that had thrived on the spirit of adventure and the burgeoning promise of mobility, the collapse of the economic boom presented an existential threat. Orders dwindled, production slowed, and the once-bustling assembly lines now hummed at a more measured pace, as the entire nation grappled with the realities of economic depression.

A Strategic Reassessment

In the face of these formidable challenges, Harley-Davidson's leadership was forced to take a hard look at their business model. The company recognized that survival in this climate required more than maintaining the status quo—it demanded strategic innovation and operational flexibility. Cost-cutting measures were introduced, and production processes were streamlined without compromising the quality that had long been the hallmark of the brand. Resources were carefully allocated, and every decision was made with a focus on sustainability.

The management team sought to balance the need for austerity with the imperative of innovation. Rather than halting progress, they explored new markets and rethought product offerings to better align with the changing economic landscape. This period of introspection and recalibration not only preserved the company during the downturn but also laid the groundwork for a renewed focus on efficiency and performance in the years to follow.

Reinvention Through Adaptation

One of the most remarkable aspects of Harley-Davidson's response to the Depression was its ability to adapt its products to suit a market in crisis. The company began to diversify its approach by developing models that were more economical to produce and operate. By refining engine designs and reducing production costs, Harley-Davidson created motorcycles that were more accessible to a broader segment of the population. This move was not just a reaction to dwindling sales—it was a proactive strategy to redefine the motorcycle as not just a luxury for the affluent but a practical, everyday mode of transportation.

In addition to product innovation, the company placed renewed emphasis on its network of dealers and service centers, nurturing relationships that could offer stability in turbulent times. The loyalty of a dedicated customer base, along with a deep-rooted connection to the brand's core values, proved invaluable. Even as economic prospects dimmed, Harley-Davidson's commitment to quality and performance reassured its patrons that the spirit of freedom could endure, no matter the circumstances.

A Testament to Resilience

The Great Depression was not merely a period of economic retrenchment—it was a crucible in which Harley-Davidson's character was forged anew. The challenges of the era necessitated a blend of prudence and innovation that ultimately strengthened the company. While many businesses faltered or vanished entirely, Harley-Davidson emerged with a hardened resolve and a leaner, more efficient operation. The hardships of the Depression underscored the importance of adaptability, a lesson that would resonate throughout the brand's subsequent history.

In the silent hum of factories and the determined faces of its workers, there was an unspoken promise: that even in the darkest of times, the call of the open road would continue to inspire. The strategies adopted during these lean years allowed Harley-Davidson not only to weather the economic storm but also to reinvent itself in ways that would secure its legacy for decades to come.

A Legacy of Endurance

Today, as we look back on the era of the Great Depression, we see a chapter that is not defined solely by economic hardship, but by a remarkable journey of resilience and reinvention. Harley-Davidson's ability to adapt to a rapidly changing world ensured that it remained true to its core promise of freedom, even when the future seemed uncertain. This legacy of endurance serves as a powerful reminder that, sometimes, the greatest triumphs are born out of the need to overcome adversity.

In surviving the storm of the Great Depression, Harley-Davidson demonstrated that true strength lies not in resisting change, but in embracing it—and in finding new ways to keep the spirit of adventure alive, no matter how fierce the storm.

o3-mini

Chapter 9: Post-War Prosperity – Rebuilding an American Icon

The conclusion of World War II ushered in an era of renewal and optimism, a time when America rebuilt not only its cities and industries but also its cultural identity. For Harley-Davidson, the post-war period was a renaissance—a chance to reassert its place as an emblem of American freedom and ingenuity. This chapter chronicles how the brand reinvented itself in a booming economy and, in doing so, became deeply intertwined with the American way of life.

A Nation on the Rise

In the wake of global conflict, the United States experienced an unprecedented economic boom. Veterans returned home eager to rebuild their lives, and with them came a surge in consumer confidence. The prosperity of the era meant that many Americans could now afford to invest in leisure and lifestyle, and Harley-Davidson was perfectly positioned to capture this newfound spirit of possibility. The motorcycles that had once roared across battlefields now began to echo on suburban roads and scenic highways, symbolizing both escape and the promise of endless adventure.

Reinventing the Brand

Harley-Davidson's transition from a wartime supplier to a peacetime icon was both swift and strategic. The company leveraged the technological innovations and manufacturing efficiencies honed during the war to produce a new generation of motorcycles. These machines combined rugged reliability with modern styling and performance enhancements, meeting the demands of an evolving market. Design elements that had been refined under the pressures of military contracts were now celebrated for their innovation and durability in the civilian realm.

The post-war models were not simply updated vehicles; they were a reimagining of what a motorcycle could be. The emphasis shifted toward comfort, ease of maintenance, and aesthetic appeal, all while preserving the distinctive character that made Harley-Davidson a symbol of rebellion and freedom. With improved engines, refined frames, and a focus on ergonomic design, these motorcycles quickly became the transport of choice for a burgeoning class of young, ambitious Americans.

Cultural Impact and the American Dream

Harley-Davidson's resurgence in the post-war years went far beyond manufacturing. The brand tapped into the zeitgeist of the era—a period marked by a renewed belief in the American Dream. As suburbs expanded and highways crisscrossed the nation, the motorcycle became more than a machine; it was a lifestyle, a statement of independence, and a symbol of self-reliance. The image of the rider on a Harley-Davidson motorcycle resonated with Americans who were eager to define their identities in a rapidly changing society.

The brand's marketing campaigns of the era captured this spirit, portraying riders as modern pioneers—individuals forging their own paths in a country filled with promise. Hollywood and popular culture embraced this image, further cementing Harley-Davidson's reputation as a beacon of American freedom. The motorcycle represented both a personal escape and a collective aspiration: the chance to explore, to discover, and to reclaim the optimism of a nation on the rise.

Building a Community

One of the most profound impacts of the post-war prosperity was the creation of a vibrant, passionate community around the Harley-Davidson brand. Riding clubs, local gatherings, and cross-country tours became common, as enthusiasts shared not only their love of the open road but also the values of independence and camaraderie that the brand embodied. This sense of community was instrumental in reinforcing the brand's image and ensured that Harley-Davidson was not merely a product but a way of life.

The company supported these initiatives by fostering relationships with dealers and by sponsoring events that celebrated the spirit of riding. Each motorcycle sold was a promise of adventure, and every ride furthered the legend of a brand that had become synonymous with the thrill of the journey. The post-war period thus saw Harley-Davidson evolve into a cultural institution—a symbol of resilience, freedom, and the collective optimism of a rebuilding nation.

Economic and Technological Transformation

The economic prosperity of the post-war era allowed Harley-Davidson to invest in research, development, and production facilities. Modern manufacturing techniques and state-of-the-art machinery began to transform the assembly lines, enabling the company to meet growing demand without sacrificing the quality and craftsmanship that had defined its legacy. This investment in technology ensured that Harley-Davidson remained competitive in a market that was rapidly embracing innovation, while still honoring the brand's storied past.

These advancements were complemented by a strategic expansion of the dealer network across the United States, making Harley-Davidson motorcycles more accessible to an ever-widening audience. The combination of improved production capabilities, savvy marketing, and a robust distribution network set the stage for a period of sustained growth that would echo throughout the decades.

The Enduring Legacy

By the close of the 1940s and into the 1950s, Harley-Davidson had firmly reestablished itself as an American icon. The post-war resurgence was not merely about bouncing back—it was about redefining what it meant to be part of the American fabric. The brand had become a mirror reflecting the nation's values: a commitment to innovation, the courage to dream big, and the unyielding pursuit of freedom.

Harley-Davidson's journey in the post-war period is a testament to its enduring spirit. It illustrates how a company, born out of necessity during times of conflict, can evolve into a cherished symbol of prosperity and individualism. The legacy of this era lives on in every Harley engine that roars to life, in every mile traveled on open highways, and in the hearts of those who see riding not just as transportation, but as a celebration of life and the American Dream.

In rebuilding itself after the war, Harley-Davidson not only contributed to the resurgence of American industry but also helped shape the cultural landscape of the nation. It stands as a reminder that even in the aftermath of conflict, the spirit of renewal and the promise of endless adventure can drive a brand—and a nation—toward a brighter future.

Chapter 10: The Rebel Years – Harley and the Counterculture Movement

The 1960s and 1970s were decades of profound social upheaval and cultural transformation in America, and at the heart of this radical shift was a spirit of rebellion—a defiant stand against conformity, authority, and the status quo. Amid this atmosphere of dissent and reinvention, Harley-Davidson motorcycles emerged as potent symbols of countercultural identity, embodying the very essence of rebellion and individual freedom.

A Catalyst for Change

In the wake of the post-war boom, society had grown increasingly complex and, to many, stifling. Traditional values were being questioned as new ideas about personal freedom, social justice, and creative expression began to flourish. Against this backdrop, the Harley-Davidson motorcycle offered more than a means of transportation—it provided a tangible expression of dissent. Its rugged design, distinctive roar, and unapologetically bold aesthetics resonated with a generation eager to break free from the constraints of a rigid, conventional society.

The Motorcycle as a Manifesto

Harley-Davidson became a moving manifesto for those who saw themselves as outsiders. In the 1960s, as young people challenged established norms in every aspect of life—from politics to music—riding a Harley was an act of defiance. The motorcycle, with its open road and unstructured journey, symbolized the possibility of an alternative lifestyle. It spoke to those who rejected the idea of being confined by predetermined paths, urging them instead to embrace uncertainty, exploration, and the pursuit of their own destiny.

This symbolism was not lost on artists, writers, and filmmakers of the era. Hollywood embraced the rebellious image of the Harley rider, immortalizing it in movies and television shows that celebrated freedom and nonconformity. The very act of riding a Harley became a statement: a bold declaration that the rider was in charge of their own destiny, unbound by societal expectations.

The Soundtrack of Rebellion

The counterculture movement found its soundtrack in the raw, unfiltered power of rock 'n' roll, and Harley-Davidson's signature engine roar fit seamlessly into this auditory rebellion. The deep rumble of a Harley became as emblematic as the electric guitar solos that defined the music of the time. This powerful association between sound and identity helped forge an emotional connection between the motorcycle and the spirit of the era. Each rev of the engine echoed the sentiments of a generation determined to redefine the boundaries of art, politics, and social interaction.

Community and the Culture of the Outlaw

Beyond its aesthetic appeal, the Harley-Davidson motorcycle fostered a unique sense of community among its riders. The counterculture was as much about shared experiences as it was about individual defiance. Riding clubs and gatherings became sanctuaries for those who identified with the ideals of rebellion. In these communities, members found solidarity and camaraderie, united by a shared disdain for societal conformity and a mutual passion for the open road.

The "outlaw" image—long associated with rugged individualism and resistance to authority—was embraced by many Harley enthusiasts. This period saw the rise of iconic biker groups that were as much about lifestyle as they were about the thrill of riding. These groups not only celebrated their independence but also provided a counterpoint to the mainstream narrative, reinforcing the motorcycle's role as a symbol of resistance.

A Lasting Impact on Identity

The legacy of the 1960s and 1970s as the Rebel Years endures in the very fabric of the Harley-Davidson brand. The motorcycle's transformation into a countercultural icon has had lasting effects on both its design philosophy and its marketing strategy. Even as society has evolved, the spirit of rebellion remains a cornerstone of Harley-Davidson's identity. Riders continue to be drawn to the promise of freedom and the allure of nonconformity—a promise that was firmly established during those turbulent, transformative decades.

In analyzing this era, it becomes clear that Harley-Davidson was not merely a product of its time but a catalyst for a cultural movement. The motorcycle, in its powerful simplicity, encapsulated the dreams and frustrations of a generation. It offered an escape from the predictable rhythms of modern life and an invitation to carve out a personal path in a rapidly changing world.

The Enduring Legacy of Rebellion

As the Rebel Years faded into history, the imprint of that defiant era remained indelible on the brand. Harley-Davidson emerged not only as an American icon of engineering excellence but also as a symbol of resistance and individualism. The rebellious spirit that defined the counterculture of the 1960s and 1970s continues to influence the ethos of Harley-Davidson today, inspiring new generations to challenge convention, pursue their passions, and, above all, ride free.

In this way, the story of Harley-Davidson during the Rebel Years is more than a chapter in the history of a motorcycle company—it is a narrative of liberation, a celebration of the power of defiance, and a testament to the enduring human desire to live life on one's own terms.

Chapter 11: The Rise of Custom Culture

By the late 20th century, the Harley-Davidson motorcycle had transcended its role as a mere mode of transportation to become a canvas for personal expression and creative innovation. As riders sought to make their machines a reflection of their own identities, a vibrant culture of customization began to take shape—a movement that would forever change the design and legacy of Harley-Davidson.

The Emergence of Personal Expression

In the early days, Harley-Davidson motorcycles were built with a focus on durability, performance, and a distinctive aesthetic that set them apart. Over time, however, enthusiasts began to view these machines not just as products, but as extensions of their personalities. Customization became a way for riders to tell their own stories—to add their personal flair to an already iconic design. This shift in perspective was fueled by a growing desire among riders to stand out in a crowd and to create a motorcycle that was uniquely their own.

As word of this trend spread, small workshops and garages began offering services that went beyond standard repairs. Skilled craftsmen and innovative mechanics started to modify everything from exhaust systems and paint jobs to engine performance and frame configurations. The motorcycle, once a uniform product emerging from assembly lines, was gradually transformed into a unique work of art—each bike a moving testament to the creativity and individuality of its owner.

A Fusion of Art and Engineering

At the heart of the custom culture was a synthesis of art and engineering. Custom builders experimented with various elements of design, blending modern technology with classic Harley aesthetics. They embraced innovations in metallurgy, composite materials, and computer-aided design to create modifications that were both visually striking and mechanically sound. These pioneers pushed the boundaries of what was possible, introducing radical ideas that challenged the conventions of motorcycle design.

The iconic rumble of a Harley was joined by a new language of style—a language expressed in intricate paintwork, chrome detailing, unique seating arrangements, and hand-fabricated parts. The custom bike, in many ways, became a mobile sculpture, where each component was chosen not only for its functionality but also for its contribution to the overall visual narrative.

This melding of form and function resonated with riders who desired more than just a means of travel; they craved a statement piece that could command attention and reflect their personal identity.

Impact on Rider Identity

For many, a custom Harley-Davidson became a powerful symbol of individuality and nonconformity. The act of customizing a motorcycle was deeply personal, an intimate process that allowed riders to mark their journey and distinguish themselves from the mainstream. As each bike was tailored to the preferences and stories of its owner, it served as an extension of their identity—a badge of honor worn on the open road.

This new era of customization also cultivated a strong sense of community among enthusiasts. Riders who customized their bikes often gathered at events, rallies, and clubs, sharing ideas, techniques, and inspiration. In these gatherings, the culture of customization flourished, fostering an environment where innovation was celebrated and individual expression was paramount. The custom bike culture not only redefined the relationship between rider and machine but also helped to solidify Harley-Davidson's reputation as a brand that champions freedom, creativity, and self-determination.

Transforming the Motorcycle Industry

The impact of the custom culture extended beyond individual expression—it also influenced the broader motorcycle industry. Harley-Davidson, recognizing the growing demand for personalization, began to embrace customization as part of its corporate identity. Limited-edition models and modular design approaches emerged, allowing buyers to select options that aligned with their personal tastes. This shift paved the way for a more interactive relationship between the manufacturer and its customers, one in which the ideas and preferences of the rider directly influenced the evolution of the product.

Moreover, the innovations developed in custom shops often trickled back into mainstream production. Techniques perfected on the fringes of the industry—ranging from engine tuning to advanced cosmetic modifications—eventually informed the design of factory models. In this way, the custom culture acted as a laboratory for experimentation, continuously challenging established norms and inspiring improvements in performance, aesthetics, and functionality.

A Lasting Legacy

Today, the spirit of customization is deeply ingrained in the Harley-Davidson brand. What began as an expression of individual creativity has grown into a vibrant subculture that continues to influence motorcycle design worldwide. Custom Harley-Davidson motorcycles remain a symbol of rebellion and self-expression, a tribute to the enduring desire to create something that is uniquely one's own.

As we look back on the rise of custom culture, it is clear that this movement was more than a trend—it was a revolution. It transformed the way riders relate to their machines and redefined the boundaries of design and engineering. The legacy of customization lives on in every modified bike that hits the road, reminding us that behind every great machine is a unique story of passion, ingenuity, and the unyielding drive to stand out from the crowd.

Chapter 12: Global Expansion – Beyond American Borders

As the roaring engines of Harley-Davidson echoed across American highways, a new chapter was unfolding—a journey that would carry the brand far beyond its national roots. The spirit of freedom that defined Harley was not confined to the United States; it resonated with riders around the world, beckoning them to embrace the open road. This chapter explores the brand's international journey, the challenges it encountered in new markets, and the cultural adaptations that ultimately cemented its status as a global icon.

The Spark of International Ambition

In the decades following its post-war resurgence, Harley-Davidson began to cast its gaze outward. Enthusiasts from Europe, Asia, Latin America, and beyond were drawn to the allure of American freedom and rugged individualism embodied by each Harley. Recognizing this growing global appeal, the company embarked on an ambitious campaign to introduce its motorcycles to an international audience. This expansion was driven not only by the promise of new markets but also by a belief that the ethos of adventure and rebellion could bridge cultural divides.

Breaking into New Markets

Entering foreign markets was not without its challenges. Each region presented its own regulatory landscapes, competitive pressures, and unique consumer preferences. In Europe, for instance, long-established motorcycle traditions and a preference for nimble, fuel-efficient machines required Harley-Davidson to carefully position its larger, more powerful bikes. In Asia, burgeoning urban centers and rapidly evolving consumer tastes meant that Harley had to adapt both its marketing strategies and product offerings. The company invested considerable time and resources in market research, establishing local partnerships and dealer networks to better understand and serve the diverse needs of its global clientele.

Navigating Cultural Differences

Cultural adaptation was key to Harley-Davidson's international success. While the core values of freedom, individualism, and adventure transcended borders, the way these ideals were expressed varied greatly from one culture to another. In Europe, Harley tapped into the continent's rich history of motorcycling as both a sport and a lifestyle, aligning its brand with the sophistication of classic design and a spirit of refined rebellion. In contrast, in emerging markets, the Harley experience was marketed as a symbol of status and a gateway to a modern, aspirational lifestyle. Marketing campaigns were tailored to local sensibilities, blending the unmistakable Harley identity with culturally resonant narratives that celebrated both heritage and innovation.

Overcoming Market Challenges

The road to global expansion was paved with obstacles that tested the brand's resilience. Stringent environmental regulations in some countries required technical modifications to reduce emissions without compromising the signature performance that Harley riders loved. Economic fluctuations and shifting consumer trends sometimes posed additional hurdles, demanding agile strategies and inventive solutions. Despite these challenges, Harley-Davidson's commitment to quality and authenticity enabled it to overcome adversity. The brand's ability to innovate—whether through redesigning components to meet local standards or launching region-specific models—ensured that it remained competitive in even the most demanding markets.

Building a Global Community

As Harley-Davidson's presence grew worldwide, it also fostered a vibrant international community of riders.

Riding clubs and events began to spring up in cities across the globe, creating spaces where enthusiasts could share their passion for the open road and celebrate the freedom that Harley symbolized. These gatherings not only reinforced brand loyalty but also highlighted the universal appeal of the motorcycle lifestyle. The shared experiences of riding, maintenance workshops, and cultural festivals transformed Harley-Davidson from a mere product into a global phenomenon—a community united by a common love for adventure and a spirit of defiance.

A Legacy Beyond Borders

Today, Harley-Davidson stands as a testament to the power of cultural adaptation and global ambition. Its international journey has been one of continuous learning and transformation. The challenges faced along the way—whether technical, regulatory, or cultural—have only enriched the brand, ensuring that each motorcycle carries not just the legacy of American freedom, but also a story of global integration and resilience.

In tracing Harley-Davidson's path beyond American borders, we see a brand that has not only conquered new markets but has also embraced the diversity of the world. Its global expansion is a reflection of an enduring promise: that the call of the open road transcends national boundaries and that the spirit of adventure is a universal language. As Harley continues to inspire riders around the globe, its journey serves as a powerful reminder that innovation, adaptability, and a commitment to core values can unite us all in the shared pursuit of freedom.

Chapter 13: The Evolution of Engine Technology

The heartbeat of every Harley-Davidson motorcycle is its engine—a symphony of precision engineering and raw power that has evolved over the decades. This chapter delves into the technical advancements and engineering milestones that have defined Harley's engine technology, tracing the journey from its humble beginnings to the high-performance machines of today.

The Genesis: A Vision for Power

In its early days, Harley-Davidson engineers were confronted with the monumental task of creating a motorized engine that could withstand the demands of long-distance travel on unpaved roads. The solution emerged in the form of the V-twin engine, a design that would come to define the Harley-Davidson legacy. Early iterations were simple in construction but revolutionary in concept—two cylinders arranged in a V configuration that delivered a distinctive balance of power and smooth operation. This design was not only robust enough for the era's rudimentary roads but also provided the kind of torque that became synonymous with the brand's raw, throaty roar.

Refining the V-Twin: Precision and Performance

As technology progressed, so too did the sophistication of Harley's engines. Through the mid-20th century, continuous refinements in metallurgy and machining allowed engineers to tighten tolerances and improve engine reliability. The introduction of advanced lubrication systems, improved fuel delivery mechanisms, and more precise ignition timing all contributed to engines that were not only more efficient but also more durable. Each innovation was a calculated response to the challenges posed by both the open road and rigorous military demands during wartime, ensuring that every Harley engine delivered consistent performance under diverse conditions.

Embracing Innovation: Technological Milestones

The evolution of Harley-Davidson's engine technology is marked by a series of groundbreaking advancements:

- **Enhanced Combustion Efficiency:** Through iterative design improvements, engineers optimized the combustion process, allowing engines to extract more power from each drop of fuel. This not only boosted performance but also contributed to a longer engine life and reduced emissions—a crucial step as environmental considerations began to shape automotive design.

- **Cooling and Thermal Management:** Early engines often struggled with overheating under prolonged use. The development of improved cooling systems, including air and liquid-cooling innovations in later years, enabled Harley engines to maintain optimal operating temperatures, ensuring reliability even in extreme conditions.

- **Electronic Advancements:** The latter part of the 20th century saw the introduction of electronic fuel injection and computerized engine management systems. These technologies revolutionized the way engines were controlled, allowing for more precise adjustments to air-fuel mixtures and ignition timing. The result was smoother acceleration, improved fuel economy, and a consistent performance that riders could rely on, regardless of the terrain.

- **Modular Design and Customization:** As customization became a cornerstone of the Harley experience, engine design evolved to offer greater flexibility. Modular components allowed riders to tailor performance characteristics to their individual preferences, paving the way for an entire subculture of performance tuning and bespoke engineering.

Balancing Heritage and Modernity

Throughout these decades of rapid innovation, Harley-Davidson has maintained a delicate balance between preserving its storied past and embracing cutting-edge technology. While modern engines boast impressive advancements in efficiency, power, and environmental performance, they still echo the distinctive sound and character of the original V-twin design. This continuity ensures that even as engines become more technologically sophisticated, they remain unmistakably Harley—a blend of tradition and innovation that resonates with riders on a deeply emotional level.

The Impact on Riding Experience

The evolution of engine technology has had a profound effect on the riding experience. Each new generation of engines has enabled Harley-Davidson motorcycles to cover greater distances with enhanced reliability, making long journeys less about overcoming mechanical obstacles and more about the thrill of the ride. The improved performance has also allowed for greater versatility, from the aggressive demands of racing circuits to the smooth, steady power required for leisurely cruises down the highway. In every case, the engine remains the core of the experience—a testament to the relentless pursuit of perfection that has driven Harley-Davidson for over a century.

A Legacy of Engineering Excellence

Looking back on the evolution of engine technology, it becomes clear that every innovation, every engineering milestone, has contributed to the indomitable spirit of Harley-Davidson. From the early, hand-crafted V-twins to today's precision-engineered powerplants, the journey of the Harley engine is a narrative of continuous improvement, resilience, and passion for performance. It is a legacy built on the belief that every mile traveled is a triumph of engineering and that the open road always beckons for more.

In this chapter, we celebrate the ingenuity and dedication of the engineers who have transformed a simple concept into a dynamic force that powers not only machines, but a cultural phenomenon. The evolution of Harley-Davidson's engine technology is more than a technical chronicle—it is a story of how relentless innovation can keep the spirit of adventure alive, one revolution at a time.

Chapter 14: Design and Aesthetics – Form Meets Function

At the intersection of art and engineering lies the essence of Harley-Davidson's enduring appeal. In an industry driven by performance, the brand's design philosophy has always placed equal value on aesthetics and functionality. This chapter examines how Harley-Davidson has maintained a timeless look while continually innovating, marrying form and function into a visual language that speaks to riders around the world.

The Power of Iconic Silhouettes

From its inception, Harley-Davidson embraced a design language that was both bold and instantly recognizable. The low-slung profile, aggressive stance, and muscular curves of early models were not merely choices of style but reflections of a philosophy that prioritized strength and durability. The silhouette of a Harley is designed to command attention on the open road—a moving piece of art that exudes confidence and power. Over the decades, while the technology beneath the fairings has evolved, the core visual identity has remained constant, reinforcing the idea that true style is timeless.

A Balance Between Heritage and Innovation

Harley-Davidson's design journey is marked by a careful balancing act between honoring its heritage and embracing modern innovation. Designers and engineers have consistently looked to the brand's storied past for inspiration, drawing on elements that evoke a sense of history and nostalgia. Yet, they have also dared to push boundaries, integrating contemporary materials, advanced manufacturing techniques, and state-of-the-art technology into new models.

For instance, while the unmistakable V-twin engine and its distinctive rumble have remained a staple, modern bikes feature refined chassis, aerodynamic enhancements, and digital instrumentation that serve today's riders without diluting the legacy of the past. The result is a motorcycle that pays homage to tradition while confidently striding into the future—a design that proves that innovation need not sacrifice identity.

Form Following Function

Every curve, every line on a Harley-Davidson is meticulously crafted with a purpose. The design process begins with engineering considerations, where every component is optimized for performance, safety, and comfort. Yet, within those constraints lies an opportunity for creative expression. Designers transform mechanical necessities into sculptural elements, turning engine covers, fenders, and frames into works of art that complement the motorcycle's rugged character.

This philosophy is evident in the thoughtful placement of controls, the ergonomic design of the seating, and the strategic use of materials that enhance both durability and aesthetic appeal. The fusion of form and function is not accidental—it is the result of an iterative process where each design element is refined to serve multiple purposes. In this way, the visual appeal of a Harley-Davidson is deeply intertwined with its performance on the road, creating an experience that is as pleasing to the eye as it is exhilarating to ride.

The Language of Customization

Customization is another key aspect of Harley-Davidson's design philosophy. The brand understands that its riders seek more than a cookie-cutter product—they desire a motorcycle that reflects their personal identity and style. This has led to a design ecosystem where modular components and customizable features are built into the very framework of the bikes. From distinctive paint schemes and chrome detailing to bespoke accessories and modified ergonomics, each Harley can be tailored to express the individuality of its owner.

This commitment to customization reinforces the notion that design is not static but an evolving conversation between the rider and the machine. As trends shift and tastes evolve, Harley-Davidson's design team remains agile, ensuring that each new model can serve as a blank canvas for the rider's own creative vision. In this ongoing dialogue, the motorcycle becomes a personal statement—a testament to the idea that beauty and performance can be uniquely combined to suit diverse lifestyles.

Enduring Aesthetics in a Changing World

Despite the rapid pace of technological change and shifting consumer preferences, Harley-Davidson's design ethos has proven remarkably resilient. The classic elements of the brand's look—the powerful stance, the interplay of light and shadow on polished metal, and the distinctive engine silhouette—continue to evoke an emotional response that transcends time. This enduring appeal is a testament to the brand's ability to tap into universal ideals of freedom, strength, and authenticity.

Design at Harley-Davidson is not merely about keeping up with trends; it is about creating a legacy that resonates with generations of riders. The company's design teams draw inspiration from diverse sources—ranging from the raw aesthetics of industrial machinery to the flowing lines of nature—ensuring that every model is both a modern marvel and a nod to the past. This holistic approach to design has enabled Harley-Davidson to craft motorcycles that are not only technologically advanced but also rich in character and soul.

A Continuous Journey of Evolution

The design and aesthetics of Harley-Davidson motorcycles are the visible manifestation of an ongoing journey—a pursuit of perfection that spans over a century. As new materials, technologies, and ideas emerge, the brand remains committed to its core values while exploring innovative ways to express them. Each new model is a chapter in a larger narrative that celebrates the union of art and engineering, where every detail is a deliberate choice that enhances the rider's experience.

In this chapter, we celebrate the design philosophies that have kept Harley-Davidson at the forefront of motorcycle culture. By ensuring that every bike is both a masterpiece of form and a marvel of function, Harley-Davidson continues to inspire riders with machines that are as aesthetically captivating as they are mechanically superior. In doing so, the brand proves that when design and engineering work in harmony, the result is a timeless icon that can weather the test of time and continue to capture the imagination of the world.

Chapter 15: Harley in Popular Culture

Harley-Davidson is more than a motorcycle manufacturer—it is a cultural phenomenon that has captured the imagination of artists, filmmakers, musicians, and writers around the world. Over the decades, the brand has transcended its utilitarian origins to become an enduring icon of freedom, rebellion, and the American spirit. This chapter explores how Harley-Davidson has been depicted in popular culture and the ways in which these portrayals have solidified its legendary status.

Hollywood and the Silver Screen

From the earliest days of cinema, Harley-Davidson motorcycles have been a favorite prop for directors seeking to convey a sense of rugged individualism and defiant spirit. In classic films of the 1950s and 1960s, the image of a lone rider blazing across vast, open landscapes came to symbolize the untamed frontier—a metaphor for breaking free from societal constraints. Movies such as THE WILD ONE and EASY RIDER cemented the motorcycle's association with counterculture and nonconformity, portraying Harley riders as rebels challenging the established order. These cinematic depictions not only enhanced the brand's allure but also contributed to the creation of a mythos that would inspire generations of enthusiasts.

The Soundtrack of Rebellion

In the realm of music, Harley-Davidson found a natural partner in the rebellious strains of rock 'n' roll and blues. The roar of a Harley engine, with its distinctive rumble, became a sonic symbol of defiance and raw power—a perfect complement to the gritty guitar riffs and pounding drums of the era. Iconic bands and musicians referenced Harley-Davidson in lyrics and imagery, with the motorcycle becoming a shorthand for a life lived on the edge. The symbiotic relationship between the brand and the music scene further propelled Harley into the public consciousness, as it came to represent not only the freedom of the open road but also the passionate, unrestrained spirit of youth culture.

Literary Legends and Cultural Narratives

Harley-Davidson's impact on popular culture is also deeply woven into literature and storytelling. Authors have long used the motorcycle as a metaphor for personal liberation, the pursuit of adventure, and the defiance of conventional paths. Memoirs and novels set against the backdrop of long, winding highways often feature Harley-

Davidson as the catalyst for transformative journeys—both physical and emotional. These narratives celebrate the motorcycle as more than a machine; it is a vessel for self-discovery and a symbol of the relentless quest for individuality. In this way, Harley-Davidson has helped shape a cultural narrative that champions the idea of the road as a place where limits are challenged and dreams are pursued.

Fashion, Art, and Lifestyle

Beyond film, music, and literature, Harley-Davidson has also permeated the worlds of fashion and art. The brand's bold logo, rugged aesthetics, and association with counterculture have inspired countless designers and visual artists. From leather jackets emblazoned with the iconic eagle and bar-and-shield emblem to murals celebrating the open road, the Harley image is ubiquitous in popular visual culture. This fusion of art and lifestyle has transformed Harley-Davidson into a symbol that people wear and display as an expression of their personal values—freedom, courage, and a disdain for the ordinary.

Enduring Symbol of Freedom

At its core, Harley-Davidson represents an enduring ideal: the unyielding desire to break free from societal confines and chart one's own course. This ideal resonates across borders and generations, making the brand a universal emblem of independence. Whether viewed on the silver screen, heard in a raucous guitar solo, read in a storied novel, or worn as a badge of honor, Harley-Davidson stands as a testament to the human spirit's longing for adventure and autonomy.

The multifaceted portrayal of Harley in popular culture has ensured that the brand remains not only relevant but also aspirational. It has evolved from a mere motorcycle manufacturer into a powerful cultural symbol—a beacon of freedom that continues to inspire and captivate the hearts of those who dare to live life on their own terms. In celebrating its legacy in film, music, literature, and art, we see that Harley-Davidson is far more than a machine; it is a living, breathing icon of the relentless pursuit of freedom.

Chapter 16: Racing and Performance – The Competitive Edge

From the very inception of its engines to its modern-day innovations, Harley-Davidson has always been driven by a passion for performance. While the brand is widely celebrated for its cultural impact and iconic design, its commitment to speed, precision, and competitive excellence has also left an indelible mark on the world of motorsports. This chapter explores Harley's storied history in racing, the relentless quest for performance, and the engineering breakthroughs that allowed the company to push the boundaries of what a motorcycle could achieve on the track.

The Early Forays into Competitive Racing

In the decades following its founding, Harley-Davidson was quick to recognize that the open road was not only a stage for leisurely rides but also a proving ground for engineering excellence. Early races and competitive events offered a platform where the durability and power of Harley's V-twin engines could be tested under extreme conditions. These formative competitions were more than just contests of speed—they were opportunities for the company's engineers to refine their designs through real-world challenges, gaining invaluable data on performance, handling, and endurance.

As the company honed its techniques on rugged test tracks and backcountry circuits, the insights gleaned from racing began to inform every facet of production. Innovations in engine tuning, frame dynamics, and suspension geometry were born from the need to win races, and each victory on the track served as a public demonstration of Harley-Davidson's commitment to excellence.

Engineering for the Fast Lane

The competitive spirit that drove Harley-Davidson on the race circuit quickly became a catalyst for technological advancement. In pursuit of ever-higher speeds and improved handling, engineers experimented with various modifications that would eventually revolutionize the design of the motorcycle. Key performance milestones included:

- **Enhanced Engine Tuning:** Through meticulous adjustments in fuel delivery, ignition timing, and exhaust flow, Harley engineers pushed the limits of the V-twin engine. These improvements not only increased horsepower and torque but also established the distinct, throaty roar that remains synonymous with the brand.

- **Lightweight, Robust Frames:** To achieve better speed and maneuverability, the design of the motorcycle's chassis underwent significant refinements. Emphasizing both strength and weight reduction, these modifications allowed for more responsive handling on tight curves and at high speeds, a critical factor in competitive racing.

- **Advanced Suspension Systems:** Racing demands precise control over every inch of the motorcycle. Harley-Davidson invested heavily in developing suspension systems that could absorb the rigors of high-speed competition while maintaining stability and comfort, allowing riders to navigate challenging tracks with confidence.

Triumphs on the Track

Harley-Davidson's racing legacy is punctuated by a series of impressive triumphs. Whether on dirt tracks, paved circuits, or in endurance challenges, Harley racers have consistently demonstrated that the brand's machines are engineered to excel under pressure. These victories not only bolstered the company's reputation among motorsports enthusiasts but also helped forge a close-knit community of riders who revered the competitive edge as much as the cultural iconography of the brand.

Racing events provided a stage where Harley-Davidson could test new ideas in a high-stakes environment. Each race served as a laboratory, with engineers and riders collaborating to identify areas for improvement. The feedback loop between competitive performance and production design helped Harley remain at the forefront of motorcycle technology, even as the industry evolved.

The Racer's Influence on the Everyday Ride

The technologies and design philosophies honed on the track found their way into the consumer models, making the everyday Harley-Davidson not only a symbol of freedom but also a product of cutting-edge performance engineering. Many of the performance innovations—be it improvements in engine reliability, braking systems, or chassis dynamics—became standard features in the motorcycles that millions of riders took to the open road. In this way, the pursuit of racing excellence had a dual benefit: it provided a competitive edge on the track and elevated the overall riding experience for Harley enthusiasts worldwide.

A Legacy of Speed and Endurance

Today, while Harley-Davidson's presence in mainstream motorsports may not dominate headlines as it once did, the competitive spirit remains an integral part of the brand's DNA. Racing is not simply a chapter in the company's history—it is a continuous source of inspiration. Modern Harley engineers still look to the lessons learned on the track as they innovate in areas such as performance tuning, lightweight materials, and advanced electronic systems. This legacy of racing and performance continues to shape the identity of the motorcycle, ensuring that every ride carries with it a hint of the adrenaline, determination, and triumph that defined those early competitive days.

In celebrating its racing heritage, Harley-Davidson not only honors its past but also lays the foundation for future innovations. The quest for speed, the commitment to engineering excellence, and the passion for competitive performance remain as relevant today as they were in the early days of motorsport. For every rider who feels the surge of power on the open road, there is a legacy of racing and performance that continues to drive the brand forward—a reminder that the competitive edge is a cornerstone of what it means to ride a Harley-Davidson.

Chapter 17: The Business of a Legend

Behind every roaring Harley engine lies not only exceptional engineering and design, but also a series of shrewd business decisions and innovative marketing strategies that have propelled the brand through cycles of boom and bust. In this chapter, we delve into the corporate acumen that transformed Harley-Davidson from a modest Milwaukee workshop into a global cultural icon, examining how brand loyalty, astute management, and forward-thinking marketing strategies sustained the company through times of both unprecedented success and challenging adversity.

Crafting a Distinctive Brand Identity

Harley-Davidson's journey began with more than just mechanical ingenuity—it was built on a distinct identity that resonated with the spirit of freedom and rebellion. Early on, the company recognized that its motorcycles were not just products, but symbols of a lifestyle. This insight drove its marketing strategies, from the very first advertisements that portrayed riders as independent and adventurous, to later campaigns that tapped into the mystique of the open road. The iconic bar-and-shield logo, coupled with the unmistakable rumble of the V-twin engine, became a powerful shorthand for American heritage and individualism. This consistent brand image not only attracted new customers but also forged deep emotional connections with existing ones, laying the foundation for extraordinary brand loyalty.

Innovative Marketing and Storytelling

Harley-Davidson's marketing strategies have long been rooted in storytelling. Rather than focusing solely on technical specifications, the company crafted narratives that celebrated the freedom of the ride and the rebel spirit of its riders. Campaigns were designed to evoke a sense of nostalgia and aspiration, drawing on themes of adventure, risk-taking, and nonconformity. Over the decades, marketing materials—from glossy magazine spreads to cinematic television commercials—presented Harley as a lifestyle choice rather than merely a mode of transportation. This narrative approach enabled the brand to transcend the boundaries of its product category, transforming each motorcycle into a symbol of personal liberation and the promise of endless adventure.

Building and Sustaining Brand Loyalty

Central to Harley-Davidson's business success has been the cultivation of an intensely loyal community of riders. This loyalty was not simply a result of quality engineering or captivating marketing—it was also fostered through the creation of a vibrant, inclusive culture. Harley's dealership networks and rider clubs evolved into more than sales outlets; they became hubs for community building, where enthusiasts shared their experiences, celebrated their victories, and offered support during hardships. This sense of belonging was further reinforced by events such as rallies, custom bike shows, and international gatherings, which provided riders with opportunities to connect with the brand and with each other. In this way, Harley-Davidson not only sold motorcycles but also nurtured a dedicated family of riders who would champion the brand across generations.

Strategic Business Decisions and Adaptability

The history of Harley-Davidson is marked by periods of both prosperity and turbulence. Economic downturns, shifts in consumer preferences, and competitive pressures tested the resilience of the company time and again. However, strategic decision-making and an adaptive business model enabled Harley to navigate these challenges successfully. During lean times, the company streamlined production, implemented cost-control measures, and refocused on its core values of quality and performance. Conversely, during periods of growth, Harley invested in expanding its production capabilities, modernizing its supply chain, and exploring new markets. These decisions were underpinned by a deep understanding of market trends and an unwavering commitment to innovation, ensuring that the brand remained both relevant and revered.

Diversification and Global Expansion

Recognizing that its appeal extended far beyond American shores, Harley-Davidson made deliberate moves to diversify its offerings and expand globally. While remaining true to its heritage, the company adapted its product lines to suit the tastes and regulatory requirements of international markets. The establishment of regional offices, partnerships with local dealers, and culturally attuned marketing campaigns allowed Harley to build a robust global presence. This international strategy not only opened new revenue streams but also reinforced the brand's status as a universal symbol of freedom and rebellion.

Navigating the Digital Age

In recent years, the rise of digital technology and social media has transformed the landscape of marketing and consumer engagement. Harley-Davidson has embraced these changes by harnessing the power of online communities, digital storytelling, and e-commerce platforms. The brand's digital initiatives have expanded its reach, allowing it to connect with a younger, tech-savvy audience while still catering to its long-standing customer base. Interactive websites, virtual events, and targeted social media campaigns have all played a role in keeping the brand's narrative fresh and engaging, ensuring that Harley continues to inspire both new and veteran riders alike.

A Legacy of Resilience and Vision

At its core, the business of Harley-Davidson is a story of resilience and visionary leadership. Through a combination of compelling storytelling, strategic market positioning, and an unwavering commitment to its core values, Harley-Davidson has not only weathered economic storms but has emerged stronger with each challenge. The company's ability to blend tradition with innovation has allowed it to maintain a commanding presence in a rapidly changing world, while its emphasis on community and culture has forged a loyal following that extends far beyond the realm of motorcycle enthusiasts.

In analyzing the business decisions and marketing strategies that have sustained Harley-Davidson through the ups and downs of the marketplace, we uncover a blueprint for enduring success—one that balances heritage with innovation, emphasizes the power of a cohesive brand identity, and prioritizes the creation of lasting emotional connections. The business of a legend is, at its heart, a testament to the idea that with vision, adaptability, and a commitment to authenticity, even the most storied brands can continue to thrive in the face of change.

Chapter 18: Challenges in the Modern Era

In recent decades, the landscape in which Harley-Davidson operates has grown increasingly complex, marked by rapid technological advancements, shifting consumer preferences, and a global marketplace that is as competitive as it is diverse. As one of America's most iconic brands, Harley-Davidson has faced a myriad of modern obstacles—each requiring the company to adapt and evolve while staying true to its storied legacy.

Globalization and Market Competition

The forces of globalization have transformed the motorcycle industry in profound ways. With the opening of markets around the world, Harley-Davidson found itself not only competing with domestic manufacturers but also with an influx of international brands offering a wide range of products at various price points. Manufacturers from Asia and Europe, with their reputation for innovative engineering and cost-effective production, began to capture significant shares of markets that were once considered exclusive to American craftsmanship.

This global competition forced Harley to rethink its approach to design, production, and distribution. The challenge lay in preserving the heritage and premium quality that defined the brand while adjusting to a marketplace characterized by leaner margins and faster product cycles. To maintain its competitive edge, Harley-Davidson had to invest in new technologies, streamline operations, and sometimes even reinvent parts of its product line to appeal to consumers in diverse economic and cultural contexts.

Regulatory Changes and Environmental Demands

Another major challenge has come from the ever-tightening web of regulations, particularly those related to environmental standards and safety. In an era where climate change and sustainability are at the forefront of public policy, regulatory bodies across the globe have imposed stricter emissions standards and safety requirements. These changes have compelled Harley-Davidson to reengineer its engines and adapt its manufacturing processes to meet new, more rigorous environmental criteria without compromising the signature performance and sound that riders love.

Adapting to these regulatory shifts has required significant investment in research and development. The integration of advanced emission control technologies, exploration of alternative fuels, and even the conceptualization of electric models are all part of Harley's response to a world where environmental responsibility is increasingly non-negotiable. Balancing the heritage of a roaring, gasoline-powered engine with the need for cleaner, greener technology is a formidable task—one that continues to challenge the company's engineers and strategists.

Shifting Consumer Tastes and Demographic Changes

Consumer preferences have evolved dramatically in the modern era. The motorcycle market, once dominated by the allure of freedom and rebellion, now contends with a new generation of riders whose tastes are influenced by digital connectivity, urban mobility, and a broader array of lifestyle choices. Younger consumers, often more environmentally conscious and financially pragmatic, have shown interest in alternative forms of personal transportation, such as electric scooters and bikes that align with urban lifestyles.

This shifting demographic landscape has forced Harley-Davidson to reconsider its market positioning. While the brand's legacy continues to attract loyal enthusiasts, capturing the attention of a younger, more diverse customer base has proven to be a complex challenge. The company has had to reexamine its product portfolio, marketing strategies, and overall brand narrative. Efforts to integrate modern design elements, incorporate smart technology, and even develop electric models are part of the broader strategy to align the Harley experience with the evolving expectations of today's consumers.

Navigating the Digital Transformation

Digital transformation has reshaped every facet of business, from marketing and sales to customer service and product development. For Harley-Davidson, embracing the digital revolution means not only leveraging social media to engage with its community but also integrating digital technologies into the motorcycle itself. The rise of connected devices, data analytics, and e-commerce platforms has altered the way the brand interacts with riders and manages its global operations.

Adapting to these changes involves significant cultural and operational shifts. Harley-Davidson has had to invest in digital infrastructure, retrain its workforce, and develop new capabilities in areas such as online customer engagement and digital supply chain management. The challenge is to harness the power of technology without losing the personal, rebellious touch that has defined the brand for over a century.

A Future of Adaptation and Innovation

Despite these modern challenges, Harley-Davidson's enduring legacy and commitment to innovation position it to navigate the turbulent waters of globalization, regulatory change, and evolving consumer tastes. The company's ongoing efforts to diversify its product range, including ventures into electric motorcycles and urban mobility solutions, signal a readiness to adapt without sacrificing the core values that have made Harley synonymous with freedom and adventure.

In the face of these obstacles, the modern era is not just a period of challenge—it is also a time of opportunity. By continuing to innovate, embracing new technologies, and listening closely to the shifting desires of a global consumer base, Harley-Davidson aims to reaffirm its status as a legendary brand for future generations. The road ahead may be complex, but with its rich heritage and unwavering spirit, Harley-Davidson is poised to ride into a future defined by resilience, adaptability, and continuous reinvention.

Chapter 19: Innovation and Tradition – A Balancing Act

In the dynamic landscape of the modern era, Harley-Davidson faces a compelling challenge: how to remain true to a century-old legacy of rebellious freedom while embracing the innovations of today. This chapter explores the delicate interplay between preserving heritage and integrating modern technology and sustainability into every facet of the brand, demonstrating that the spirit of a Harley rider is as much about honoring the past as it is about steering confidently into the future.

Honoring a Storied Past

For decades, Harley-Davidson has built its identity on a foundation of unmistakable design, robust engineering, and an ethos of unbridled individualism. The familiar rumble of a V-twin engine, the iconic bar-and-shield logo, and the distinctive silhouette of its motorcycles evoke memories of open highways and rebellious spirit. These elements are more than aesthetics; they serve as a bridge to a storied past that continues to resonate with loyal riders.

At its core, Harley-Davidson is not merely a product—it is a cultural symbol. The brand's longstanding tradition of celebrating freedom and adventure is woven into every machine and every marketing narrative. Even as technology evolves, Harley-Davidson remains dedicated to preserving the soul of its classic designs, ensuring that each new model retains a connection to the legacy that made the brand an enduring icon.

Embracing Modern Technology

While reverence for tradition is a hallmark of Harley-Davidson, innovation is equally integral to its survival and growth. The company has invested significantly in modernizing its production techniques, incorporating advanced manufacturing technologies and digital tools to enhance precision and efficiency. These technological advancements have led to improvements in engine performance, safety features, and overall ride quality without diluting the brand's unmistakable character.

For example, modern Harley models now feature digital instrumentation, electronic fuel injection, and integrated connectivity solutions that allow riders to customize their riding experience. These innovations not only enhance performance and reliability but also appeal to a new generation of tech-savvy riders. By blending state-of-the-art technology with classic design elements, Harley-Davidson creates machines that are both high-performing and steeped in tradition.

Sustainability: A New Frontier

In an era increasingly defined by environmental awareness, sustainability has become a key focus for manufacturers across all industries. For Harley-Davidson, integrating sustainability into its operations and product development is not just about meeting regulatory requirements—it's about ensuring that the spirit of freedom endures in a world that values environmental responsibility.

The company has taken meaningful strides to reduce its ecological footprint, from adopting greener manufacturing practices to exploring alternative energy sources. One notable development is Harley's venture into electric motorcycles. While these models represent a significant technological shift, they are designed to honor the brand's signature aesthetic and riding experience. The challenge has been to engineer electric powertrains that deliver the distinctive performance and soulful roar associated with Harley while offering a cleaner, more sustainable option for modern riders.

The Synthesis of Old and New

The art of balancing innovation with tradition is evident in every aspect of Harley-Davidson's approach. Product development teams work in close collaboration with historians and designers who understand the brand's legacy, ensuring that new models incorporate modern enhancements without erasing the elements that longtime enthusiasts cherish. This synthesis is not merely about preserving history—it's about evolving that history to remain relevant in an ever-changing world.

Marketing and branding strategies further underscore this balance. Promotional campaigns highlight the rich heritage of Harley-Davidson even as they introduce cutting-edge features and sustainability initiatives. The narrative is one of continuous evolution: a brand that honors its past while actively shaping its future. This duality resonates with a diverse audience, bridging the gap between nostalgic riders and those seeking innovative, sustainable solutions for contemporary lifestyles.

Looking Ahead

As Harley-Davidson moves forward, its commitment to blending tradition with innovation sets a powerful example for how legacy brands can thrive in modern times. The company's journey is a testament to the belief that honoring one's roots does not preclude embracing the new; rather, it can serve as a catalyst for creative reinvention. By maintaining a dialogue between heritage and technology, Harley-Davidson ensures that each motorcycle is not only a tribute to its illustrious past but also a bold statement of progress and sustainability.

In this balancing act, Harley-Davidson continues to inspire riders around the world. Every modern model tells a story—of resilience, evolution, and the enduring pursuit of freedom. It is a story that seamlessly merges the timeless allure of its classic designs with the promise of innovation, proving that the spirit of a Harley is as relevant today as it ever was.

Chapter 20: The Rider's Legacy – Stories from the Road

Harley-Davidson isn't just built in factories or defined by its roaring engines; it lives in the hearts and memories of the riders who have taken to the open road. This chapter is a tribute to the countless personal narratives, candid interviews, and unforgettable anecdotes shared by Harley enthusiasts around the globe. These stories, varied in tone and origin, weave together a rich tapestry that reflects the true spirit of the Harley community—a legacy forged in the freedom of the ride.

A Tapestry of Tales

From the dusty backroads of the American Midwest to the winding mountain passes of Europe and the sun-drenched highways of Australia, every rider's journey tells a unique story. Many speak of the transformative power of the open road—a journey that began with a simple ignition and evolved into a lifelong passion. One such rider, Tom, a retired veteran from Texas, recalls his first ride on a vintage Harley:

"The moment I twisted the throttle, it felt like every worry and burden melted away. It wasn't just about getting from point A to point B—it was about feeling alive, in tune with the road and with my own soul."

Tom's story resonates with countless riders who have discovered that a Harley is more than a machine—it's an extension of one's identity.

Voices of the Open Road

In a series of candid interviews, riders from different backgrounds share what it means to be part of the Harley family. Maria, a young professional from Barcelona, speaks of her first cross-country adventure:

"I always thought motorcycles were reserved for a certain kind of rebel. But riding my Harley taught me that it's about empowerment and self-discovery. The wind in your face, the endless horizon—it forces you to embrace life's unpredictability."

Another rider, Kenji from Tokyo, highlights the global nature of the Harley experience:

"I joined a local rider club, and soon I was connecting with fellow enthusiasts from all corners of the world. Our rides have taken us through bustling cities and serene countrysides, and every journey deepens the bond we share. It's a language of freedom that transcends borders."

Anecdotes That Define a Lifestyle

Anecdotes often capture the spirit of Harley-Davidson in ways that statistics and technical specifications cannot. There's the legendary story of a group ride in the Rocky Mountains, where a sudden storm forced riders to band together. One rider, known as "Dusty," recounted how the group found shelter in a remote cabin:

"We were strangers from different parts of the country, yet in that moment, sharing stories over hot coffee by a crackling fire, we were a family. That day, the storm reminded us that no matter where the road takes us, we're all connected by the same passion."

Similarly, during an international rally in New Zealand, a seasoned rider named Fiona shared how the experience redefined her sense of belonging:

"The rally wasn't just a gathering—it was a celebration of every mile we've conquered. I met people who had journeyed thousands of kilometers, each with a tale as wild and winding as the roads we rode. It was humbling and inspiring all at once."

The Legacy Lives On

For many, these stories are not just memories but living legacies passed down from one generation to the next. Older riders often mentor newcomers, sharing tips about maintenance, route planning, and the subtle art of navigating not just roads, but life itself. In one heartfelt conversation at a regional meet-up in Milwaukee, an elder rider recounted:

"I remember when I first bought my Harley. It wasn't just a purchase—it was the beginning of a journey that has given me lifelong friends and adventures I never dreamed possible. Now, when I see younger riders with that same spark in their eyes, I know the legacy is secure."

Celebrating the Collective Journey

Every story shared—from the quiet reflections of solitary rides at dawn to the exuberant cheers at rally meet-ups—contributes to a collective narrative that is as diverse as it is unified. Harley-Davidson is more than a brand; it is a living, breathing community. These personal narratives form the backbone of the Harley legacy, capturing the essence of what it means to be free, to be adventurous, and to be part of something larger than oneself.

In this chapter, the rider's legacy comes alive through voices from the road—each anecdote, each shared moment of triumph and camaraderie, reaffirming that the true spirit of Harley-Davidson lives on in the hearts of its riders. As new generations take to the highways and byways, they add their own chapters to this ever-growing story—a story of passion, perseverance, and the relentless pursuit of freedom.

Chapter 21: Collecting and Preserving a Cultural Treasure

Long before social media and digital archives, a passionate community of enthusiasts recognized that Harley-Davidson was more than a motorcycle—it was a living piece of history. Today, collectors, museums, and restoration experts work tirelessly to preserve the legacy of this iconic brand, ensuring that its rich heritage endures for future generations. This chapter delves into the world of Harley collectors, the institutions dedicated to safeguarding its history, and the restoration efforts that transform vintage machines into timeless treasures.

The Passion of the Collector

For many, collecting Harley-Davidson motorcycles is a pursuit born out of deep admiration for American ingenuity and rebellious spirit. Collectors are drawn to these machines not just as investments, but as personal artifacts that capture the evolution of a cultural icon. Every bike in a collection tells its own story—from the early models built in modest Milwaukee workshops to the high-performance marvels that once raced on world-renowned circuits. Enthusiasts meticulously research serial numbers, trace production histories, and scour auction houses and private sales in search of rare examples that embody a particular era of the brand's development.

Collectors often form tight-knit communities, sharing stories of discovery, restoration challenges, and the thrill of uncovering a long-forgotten piece of Harley history. These gatherings, whether at regional meets or international rallies, serve as both a forum for exchange and a celebration of the craftsmanship that goes into every Harley. In this way, the act of collecting becomes a living homage to the brand—a means of preserving not only the physical machines but also the narratives that make them legendary.

Museums: Halls of Heritage

Around the world, museums and dedicated exhibitions play a pivotal role in preserving Harley-Davidson's storied past. Institutions like the Harley-Davidson Museum in Milwaukee serve as cultural sanctuaries where history is displayed alongside innovation. Visitors to these museums can explore meticulously curated collections of motorcycles, artifacts, and memorabilia that span the entire timeline of the brand—from its humble beginnings to its modern-day reinventions.

Exhibits often highlight the artistry and engineering behind each model, offering insights into how Harley-Davidson motorcycles have influenced American culture and inspired generations of riders. Interactive displays, archival photographs, and restored prototypes allow visitors to experience firsthand the evolution of design, technology, and marketing strategies that have kept the brand at the forefront of motorcycling. By preserving these tangible pieces of history, museums ensure that the legacy of Harley-Davidson continues to educate and inspire, serving as a bridge between past innovations and future aspirations.

Restoration: Reviving the Glory Days

Central to the preservation of Harley-Davidson's heritage is the art of restoration. Skilled craftsmen and restoration experts dedicate their careers to reviving vintage Harleys, painstakingly repairing and, when necessary, recreating original components to return these machines to their former glory. Restoration is as much an art as it is a technical discipline—a delicate balance of maintaining authenticity while ensuring that the motorcycle remains operable and safe for modern use.

The restoration process often begins with extensive research. Experts scour historical records, original blueprints, and firsthand accounts to capture every detail of the motorcycle's original design. Parts that are no longer in production may be recreated using modern manufacturing techniques that honor traditional methods, ensuring that every rivet, engine component, and chrome finish reflects the craftsmanship of a bygone era. For collectors and restoration enthusiasts alike, the journey of reviving a classic Harley is a labor of love—an act of preservation that keeps the spirit of the past alive.

The Cultural Impact of Preservation

Preserving Harley-Davidson is about more than safeguarding a collection of machines—it is about maintaining a cultural legacy. These motorcycles represent a unique chapter in the American narrative, embodying ideals of freedom, innovation, and defiance. Every restored bike, every carefully preserved exhibit, adds a new layer to the collective memory of what Harley-Davidson means to so many people.

Through restoration projects, collectors and museums not only conserve the physical artifacts but also the stories behind them. Oral histories, personal letters, and anecdotal accounts often accompany restored models, providing context and enriching the historical tapestry. This dedication to preservation ensures that future generations will not only witness the evolution of motorcycle technology but also understand the profound cultural significance behind each roaring engine and gleaming chrome detail.

A Living Legacy

Today, the world of Harley collectors, museums, and restoration experts stands as a testament to the enduring allure of this cultural treasure. Their efforts remind us that Harley-Davidson is more than a brand—it is a living archive of American innovation, resilience, and the unyielding pursuit of freedom. Each restored motorcycle and every exhibit in a museum is a celebration of the brand's journey, a journey that has captivated hearts and minds around the globe.

In preserving these timeless machines, the collective work of enthusiasts, historians, and craftsmen ensures that the legacy of Harley-Davidson will continue to inspire and enthrall. The story of Harley is not confined to the past; it is an ever-evolving narrative that lives on every time a rider takes to the open road, echoing the passion and commitment of those dedicated to keeping the spirit of Harley-Davidson alive.

Chapter 22: Customization and Community – The Harley Family

The Harley-Davidson experience extends far beyond the machine itself. It is defined by a vibrant, interconnected community where individual creativity and collective passion merge. In this chapter, we explore how custom builders, motorcycle clubs, and a myriad of events serve as the heartbeat of the Harley family, keeping the spirit of innovation and camaraderie alive across generations.

The Art of Customization

Customization is at the core of what makes a Harley-Davidson truly personal. What began as simple modifications in local garages has evolved into a sophisticated art form where riders transform their motorcycles into unique expressions of identity and creativity. Custom builders are both artisans and engineers, blending traditional techniques with modern technology to reinterpret classic designs. They painstakingly modify every element—from engine tuning and exhaust systems to bespoke paint jobs and handcrafted accessories—so that no two Harleys are ever alike.

This culture of personalization isn't driven solely by aesthetics; it's a way for riders to connect with the heritage of the brand while expressing their individuality. Customization empowers enthusiasts to tell their own stories. Whether it's a nod to vintage style or a bold leap into futuristic design, each custom bike reflects the personality of its owner and the creative energy of the community that supports them.

Clubs and Brotherhood

At the heart of the Harley-Davidson experience lies a robust network of clubs and riding groups that transcend geographic boundaries. These clubs, formed through shared passion and mutual respect for the open road, create a sense of belonging that is as enduring as the roar of a Harley engine. From local riding groups that meet for weekly rides to large, organized clubs with international memberships, these communities offer support, friendship, and a shared commitment to the values of freedom, independence, and adventure.

Membership in a Harley club is more than just riding together—it's about forging lifelong bonds. Riders share maintenance tips, organize charity events, and celebrate milestones together. The clubs are living extensions of the brand, often organizing events that bring together people from all walks of life to celebrate their love for the open road. This enduring sense of brotherhood and sisterhood is a cornerstone of the Harley-Davidson legacy.

Celebrations on the Open Road

Harley-Davidson events are more than gatherings—they are festivals of freedom that highlight the best of what the brand represents. Iconic rallies such as Sturgis, Daytona Bike Week, and local regional meets have become pilgrimage sites for enthusiasts. At these events, the roads come alive with hundreds or even thousands of custom Harleys, each one a testament to the creativity and spirit of its owner.

These rallies offer a unique blend of competition, camaraderie, and celebration. They provide custom builders with a stage to showcase their masterpieces, while also serving as opportunities for riders to network, share experiences, and learn from one another. Workshops, live demonstrations, and vendor exhibitions at these events underscore the innovative drive behind Harley-Davidson's legacy. The shared energy and passion experienced at these gatherings inspire new generations of riders to join the movement and contribute to its vibrant evolution.

The Digital Community

In the modern era, the Harley family has expanded beyond physical clubs and events to include a thriving digital community. Online forums, social media groups, and dedicated websites have created virtual spaces where riders can exchange ideas, share custom designs, and organize meet-ups. This digital connectivity has allowed the Harley spirit to transcend traditional boundaries, fostering relationships between riders from different cultures and continents.

These online communities not only serve as a repository of technical knowledge and creative inspiration, but they also play a crucial role in preserving the narrative of the Harley lifestyle. Through shared photos, video stories, and interactive discussions, the digital Harley family keeps the spirit of customization and adventure alive, ensuring that the legacy of freedom remains a living, evolving phenomenon.

The Enduring Impact of a Community-Driven Culture

The interplay between customization and community has reinforced the strength of the Harley-Davidson brand for over a century. As riders personalize their machines and share their stories with like-minded enthusiasts, they contribute to a collective legacy that is as dynamic as it is enduring. The Harley family, bound by a shared love for the open road, continuously reinvents what it means to be free, creative, and daring in a world that is ever-changing.

Through clubs, events, custom projects, and digital connections, the Harley community remains an essential part of the brand's identity. It is a living testament to the idea that a motorcycle is never just a mode of transport— it is a canvas for expression, a catalyst for friendship, and a symbol of the relentless pursuit of adventure. In celebrating this vibrant culture, Harley-Davidson not only preserves its storied past but also inspires a future where the spirit of the ride continues to unite and empower enthusiasts around the globe.

Chapter 23: Cultural Impact – A Symbol of American Freedom

Few brands capture the imagination of a nation—and indeed the world—as powerfully as Harley-Davidson. More than just a motorcycle manufacturer, Harley has become an enduring symbol of American freedom and individualism. Its influence stretches well beyond the realm of transportation, impacting art, music, fashion, and even political discourse. This chapter examines how Harley-Davidson has shaped American identity and contributed to global perceptions of freedom, rebellion, and the open road.

The American Dream on Two Wheels

Harley-Davidson emerged during an era when America was defined by a spirit of exploration and reinvention. The motorcycle quickly evolved into a metaphor for the American Dream—a vehicle for self-determination and escape from societal constraints. Riding a Harley came to represent a rejection of conformity and an embrace of personal liberty. This transformation from a mere machine into an icon of freedom was fueled by the post-war economic boom and the cultural shifts of the mid-20th century, when Americans increasingly sought to break free from traditional roles and explore new horizons.

Shaping National Identity

The rugged, rebellious image of the Harley-Davidson rider became a visual shorthand for American strength and individualism. The brand's portrayal in films, literature, and advertising helped cement its status as an emblem of nonconformity. In movies like EASY RIDER and THE WILD ONE, Harley riders were depicted as mavericks challenging social norms and asserting their independence. Such cultural representations resonated with audiences and contributed to a broader narrative about what it means to be American—bold, free-spirited, and willing to forge one's own path.

Global Perceptions of Freedom

Harley-Davidson's impact is not confined to the United States; its legacy has been exported around the globe. For international audiences, the Harley rider often symbolizes an ideal of unbounded freedom—a life where one can leave behind the constraints of modern society and embrace adventure. The distinctive sound of a Harley engine, the classic design elements, and the open-road imagery evoke a sense of liberation that transcends cultural boundaries. In many parts of the world, owning or riding a Harley has come to embody the dream of breaking free from everyday limitations, reinforcing the idea that freedom is universal.

Influence on Arts and Popular Culture

The cultural impact of Harley-Davidson is vividly evident in art, music, and fashion. Musicians have long referenced Harley in lyrics, using the motorcycle as a metaphor for rebellion and nonconformity. In visual arts, the brand's logo and iconic designs are celebrated as symbols of an era defined by both grit and glamour. Fashion, too, has embraced the Harley aesthetic—leather jackets, bandanas, and rugged boots are staples that echo the brand's ethos. These cultural expressions are not merely imitative; they actively contribute to the mythology surrounding Harley-Davidson, reinforcing its status as a cultural touchstone that encapsulates the essence of American freedom.

Political and Social Resonance

Throughout its history, Harley-Davidson has also played a role in broader political and social conversations. The motorcycle has been a symbol in protests, rallies, and movements that champion personal liberty and resistance to government overreach. Whether as an emblem of counterculture in the 1960s or as a representation of rugged individualism in more recent political discourse, Harley-Davidson's image has been harnessed to communicate ideals of autonomy, defiance, and the right to choose one's own destiny. This duality—of being both a product of its time and a timeless symbol—has enabled Harley to maintain relevance even as societal values evolve.

A Legacy of Enduring Inspiration

Harley-Davidson's cultural impact is not solely measured by its influence on consumer behavior or market trends—it is defined by its ability to inspire. The motorcycle represents the open road, the call of adventure, and the courage to pursue a life unbound by convention. For many, a Harley is more than a mode of transportation; it is a lifelong commitment to living on one's own terms. This enduring appeal continues to resonate, as new generations of riders are drawn to the brand's message of freedom and possibility.

In sum, Harley-Davidson's imprint on American culture and global perceptions of freedom is profound and multifaceted. It has helped shape an image of America that is both aspirational and rebellious—a country that values innovation, individualism, and the relentless pursuit of adventure. As a cultural icon, Harley-Davidson stands as a testament to the idea that the spirit of freedom is not just an abstract ideal but a living, roaring force that continues to inspire and transform lives around the world.

Chapter 24: The Future of Harley-Davidson

As the horizon of transportation continues to evolve, so too does the legendary brand of Harley-Davidson. Standing at the crossroads of heritage and modernity, Harley is charting a course toward a future defined by innovation, sustainability, and a reimagined riding experience. In this chapter, we explore the upcoming trends, technological breakthroughs, and strategic initiatives that will shape the next era of Harley-Davidson.

Embracing the Electric Revolution

One of the most significant shifts on the automotive horizon is the transition toward electric mobility, and Harley-Davidson is no exception. With growing environmental concerns and stricter emissions regulations worldwide, the company has recognized the importance of sustainable innovation. In recent years, Harley has taken bold steps into the realm of electric motorcycles, developing models that aim to preserve the brand's distinctive character while offering a cleaner, quieter, and more efficient ride. These new models are not merely adaptations but represent a strategic rethinking of powertrain technology, battery performance, and energy management systems. The electric Harley aims to capture a new generation of riders—those who value sustainability as much as the thrill of the ride.

Integrating Advanced Connectivity

The future of riding is not only electric but also smart. With rapid advancements in connectivity and digital technology, Harley-Davidson is exploring ways to integrate advanced features into its motorcycles. From onboard diagnostics and real-time performance analytics to integrated navigation and augmented reality displays, these innovations are poised to enhance the rider experience dramatically. The company is investing in digital ecosystems that allow riders to customize settings, track maintenance schedules, and even connect with a global community of enthusiasts through dedicated apps and online platforms. This focus on connectivity ensures that every ride becomes part of a larger, interactive journey—one that blends the physical and digital worlds seamlessly.

Redefining the Riding Experience

While technological innovation is key, Harley-Davidson remains deeply committed to the core ethos of freedom and individuality that has defined the brand for over a century. Future models are expected to marry cutting-edge engineering with the timeless design elements that Harley riders cherish. New chassis materials, improved aerodynamic profiles, and enhanced safety features will work in tandem with traditional styling cues, ensuring that each motorcycle is both a marvel of modern engineering and a nod to the legacy of the past. This synthesis of old and new is essential for appealing to both loyal long-time riders and a younger demographic seeking innovative, sustainable, and stylish alternatives.

Global Market Adaptation

The future of Harley-Davidson is also being shaped by its approach to a rapidly changing global marketplace. As emerging economies grow and consumer tastes evolve, the brand is expanding its product lines to cater to diverse markets. This involves tailoring designs, features, and price points to meet the unique demands of various regions without compromising the core identity of Harley. By forging strategic partnerships with local dealers, investing in market research, and even exploring collaborations with technology companies, Harley-Davidson is positioning itself to remain relevant and competitive on a global scale.

A Vision of Continuous Reinvention

Ultimately, the future of Harley-Davidson is characterized by an enduring commitment to reinvention. In a world where innovation is constant, the brand's willingness to adapt while staying true to its roots is what will propel it forward. As Harley embraces electric power, digital connectivity, and global diversification, it also continues to honor the rebellious spirit and craftsmanship that have long defined its legacy. The journey ahead promises to be as exciting as it is unpredictable, and with every new innovation, Harley-Davidson reaffirms its place as an icon of freedom in an ever-changing world.

In this chapter, we see that the future of Harley-Davidson is not just about keeping pace with change—it is about leading it, riding boldly into tomorrow while preserving the heart and soul of what it means to be a Harley rider.

Chapter 25: Epilogue – Riding Into Tomorrow

As the sun sets on a long and storied journey, the roar of a Harley-Davidson engine continues to echo, a timeless call to adventure that transcends generations. In this final chapter, we reflect on the legacy that has been forged over more than a century—a legacy built on innovation, rebellion, and the unwavering spirit of freedom—and look forward to the uncharted roads that lie ahead.

A Journey Etched in Time

Harley-Davidson's history is a tapestry woven with grit, ingenuity, and the dreams of countless riders who have dared to defy convention. From the modest beginnings in a Milwaukee workshop to the global phenomenon it is today, every mile traversed has added a new layer to the brand's mythos. The machines that once served as tools of war, symbols of counterculture, and canvases for personal expression now stand as living relics of American determination. They remind us that every journey—no matter how challenging—is an opportunity to push the limits of what is possible.

The Heartbeat of a Community

At the core of Harley-Davidson's enduring success is a community of riders, customizers, collectors, and dreamers. Their shared experiences, stories from the road, and unwavering loyalty have transformed a brand into a family. Whether gathered at rallies, connected through digital platforms, or united by the common thrill of the ride, these individuals carry forward the spirit of freedom that defines every Harley. It is this collective passion that ensures the legacy of Harley-Davidson will continue to thrive, inspiring future generations to embrace the open road with both reverence and daring.

Embracing Change Without Losing Essence

As we look to tomorrow, the horizon is illuminated by possibilities both familiar and novel. New technologies, sustainable innovations, and evolving consumer values are reshaping the landscape of transportation. Yet, amid the rapid pace of change, the soul of Harley-Davidson remains steadfast. The electric models, digital integrations, and global adaptations of the future are not departures from the past but extensions of a legacy that has always balanced tradition with progress. The essence of Harley—its distinctive design, its rumbling engines, its call to freedom—continues to serve as a beacon for those who believe that the journey is as important as the destination.

Imagining the Next Chapter

The road ahead is a blank canvas, inviting riders and innovators alike to contribute to the next chapter in Harley-Davidson's storied history. As we stand at the crossroads of tradition and transformation, we are reminded that every new beginning is built on the foundations of perseverance, creativity, and the courage to dream. Future models will carry forward the timeless roar of the past while integrating cutting-edge technology and sustainable practices that promise to redefine the riding experience for a new era.

Imagine a world where the unmistakable spirit of Harley-Davidson is interwoven with innovations that make every ride cleaner, smarter, and more connected—yet still deeply personal and unyielding in its call to adventure. In this future, the legacy of Harley-Davidson is not just preserved in museums or whispered in stories from the road; it lives vibrantly in every rider's heart, in every custom bike that reflects individual passion, and in every community that gathers to celebrate the unending quest for freedom.

A Farewell and a Promise

As we close this chronicle of Harley-Davidson's illustrious past, we also open the door to its limitless future. This epilogue is not a goodbye—it is an invitation to imagine, to dream, and to ride into tomorrow with the same fearless spirit that has defined Harley for over a century. The legacy of this iconic brand is as enduring as the open road itself, and its next chapter is waiting to be written by those bold enough to seize it.

So, as you turn the page, let the roar of a Harley-Davidson engine remind you that the journey is eternal, the spirit of adventure undying, and the call of freedom forever inviting. Ride on, into tomorrow.

About the Author

Etienne Psaila, an accomplished author with over two decades of experience, has mastered the art of weaving words across various genres. His journey in the literary world has been marked by a diverse array of publications, demonstrating not only his versatility but also his deep understanding of different thematic landscapes. However, it's in the realm of automotive literature that Etienne truly combines his passions, seamlessly blending his enthusiasm for cars with his innate storytelling abilities.

Specializing in automotive and motorcycle books, Etienne brings to life the world of automobiles through his eloquent prose and an array of stunning, high-quality color photographs. His works are a tribute to the industry, capturing its evolution, technological advancements, and the sheer beauty of vehicles in a manner that is both informative and visually captivating.

A proud alumnus of the University of Malta, Etienne's academic background lays a solid foundation for his meticulous research and factual accuracy. His education has not only enriched his writing but has also fueled his career as a dedicated teacher. In the classroom, just as in his writing, Etienne strives to inspire, inform, and ignite a passion for learning.

As a teacher, Etienne harnesses his experience in writing to engage and educate, bringing the same level of dedication and excellence to his students as he does to his readers. His dual role as an educator and author makes him uniquely positioned to understand and convey complex concepts with clarity and ease, whether in the classroom or through the pages of his books.

Through his literary works, Etienne Psaila continues to leave an indelible mark on the world of automotive literature, captivating car enthusiasts and readers alike with his insightful perspectives and compelling narratives.

Visit www.etiennepsaila.com for more.